# DIVORCE Care ®

25 years nnn

Left 8/24/2019   z yen
                      2 moth
Divorce 10/25/2021

6/12/2024
      3 years
      Divorce

5 years
Left

Second printing of fourth edition, October MMXXI.



CONTACT INFORMATION

Church Initiative
PO Box 1739
Wake Forest, NC 27588-1739

Phone: 800-489-7778 (US and Canada); 919-562-2112 (local and international)
Email: **info@divorcecare.org**, **info@churchinitiative.org**
Web: **divorcecare.org**, **churchinitiative.org**

CHURCH INITIATIVE: PROVIDING HELP FOR HURTING PEOPLE

Church Initiative, DivorceCare's parent ministry, offers other support group resources to help people through life's challenges. GriefShare is a grief recovery program to help people grieving the death of a loved one. DivorceCare for Kids is a 13-week program for children of separation or divorce to learn how to manage their emotions, communicate with their parents, and find hope in the confusion. To learn more, use the contact information above. We'd love to hear from you!

# Welcome

It may not have been an easy decision to join this DivorceCare group. But stick with it, and you'll be glad you did. And know that we're here to walk alongside you during what may be the hardest situation you've ever faced.

In this group, you'll discover how helpful it is to be around people who understand what you're going through. You'll also hear new information and advice that can help you heal from your separation or divorce. In fact, you'll hear things that can help you put all the pieces of your life back together.

We're sure you have more questions about the group. And your group leader will be glad to answer them. But, in the spirit of making just one thing in your life a bit easier, here are answers to some of the most common questions new group members have:

**Q: What is DivorceCare?**

A: In the coming weeks, you'll become part of a support group (one of thousands meeting around the world) where people find healing and hope after a marriage breakup. You'll be encouraged along the way by people who have been where you are. And you'll learn how to deal with your emotions and stresses and will gain tools for forward movement and health in your life.

**Q: It's my first time at DivorceCare. What's going to happen?**

A: Each week you'll view a video seminar on a divorce-related topic. The videos feature respected counselors and teachers who offer insights on how to handle the challenges you're facing. You'll also hear from people who've gone through a marriage breakup themselves—they share what has helped them. After the video, you'll discuss the concepts on the video and how they apply to you. Your DivorceCare leader will moderate the discussion time.

**Q: I'm very nervous about being here. Is this normal?**

A: You're not the only one feeling this way! Most people in your group were likely nervous the first time they came. We encourage you to commit to attending for at least three weeks; that will give you time to make a good decision about whether this group will help you. Other people have said that the support, resources, and healing found in DivorceCare far outweighed their initial anxieties.

**Q: Will I have to talk during the group?**

A: The decision to share is yours. You will benefit by listening to the videos and the discussion. Your group facilitator will encourage you to share when you are ready, because talking through your struggles and growth is instrumental in your healing.

**Q: Why do I need this workbook?**

A: The workbook is an invaluable part of your growth and healing process. You'll use the video outline to take notes during the videos. Then, during the week, you'll find short, daily exercises to help you sort through your emotions, deal with your personal situation, and find answers to your questions. Many participants also use their workbooks as a way to see how much they've healed and grown throughout the 13 weeks.

**Q: I'm not a Christian. Will DivorceCare still help me?**

A: Yes. People from all belief systems (and people who do not practice a faith) tell us that even though they are not Christians, they have found their DivorceCare groups to be wonderfully beneficial. That's because the courses are filled with practical tips on how to recover from the pain of divorce. So even if you practice another faith, or don't have any faith at all, you'll get a lot of helpful advice.

# Access your free resources

## HELP & DIRECTION WHEN YOU NEED THEM

**DIVORCECARE.ORG/MY**

# Free online help from DivorceCare

 **View the DivorceCare session videos**
Watch again or catch up on those you missed.

 **Activate your daily emails**
Sign up for "One Day at a Time," 365 days of encouragement.

 **Discover bonus content**
View bonus videos from your favorite experts and personal stories.

 **Access classic videos**
See entire past editions of DivorceCare.

 **Get holiday help**
Find tips to help you through the Thanksgiving and Christmas season.

## Gain access today!

**DIVORCECARE.ORG/MY**

# CONTENTS

# HOW DIVORCECARE HELPS YOU

You're facing what is probably the most painful experience of your life. You need support, answers, and helpful direction. You need a safe place to ask questions, share experiences, and begin to heal.

You're in the right place. DivorceCare is designed with all of these needs in mind.

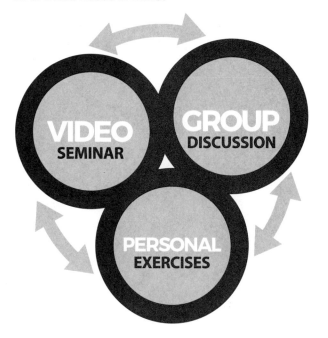

**Video seminar** – Each week you'll watch a 30-minute video with sound advice and helpful insights on managing emotions and divorce-related stresses.

**Group discussion** – After the video, you'll discuss with other group members what you learned from the video and how it applies to your circumstances.

**Personal exercises** – You'll receive a DivorceCare book filled with purposeful articles and exercises to help you move through the healing process.

At DivorceCare you'll meet other people who "get" what you're going through, because they've been there too. And you'll have a strategy for overcoming the emotional roller coaster of divorce. More specifically, you'll:

- Find healthy ways to deal with loneliness
- Gain control of your anger
- Learn to communicate more effectively with your ex and others
- Grow in confidence and peace
- Get a better handle on your emotions

And like the thousands of others who have turned to DivorceCare for support, you'll find hope for the future.

*"DivorceCare was a powerful tool in my healing process."* – Jennifer

# GROUP GUIDELINES

It's important for a DivorceCare group to be a place where people feel safe, welcomed, and accepted. The most beneficial groups establish guidelines that members are committed to following and that are in the best interests of the members. Your group will develop its own guidelines, but here are some suggestions:

## Share

There is no requirement to talk or share in the group, but you're encouraged to do so! There is great healing in being able to share your journey with others who really understand and care. But remember, if you tend to be a "talker," there are other people in the group who need to share too, so don't dominate the discussion time.

## Listen

Be willing to listen. When someone else is speaking, focus on what that person is saying in order to learn, comfort, and help. Good listening builds relationships. Remember to refrain from cross talk (talking while someone else is talking).

## Give and receive advice cautiously

As a general rule during the group, the best time to give advice is when someone asks for it. If someone requests your input, don't insist that person takes your suggestion or responds to issues in the same way you have. Also remember, the advice you receive from fellow group members may not be appropriate in your circumstances. Carefully evaluate the suggestions you receive.

## Complete your participant guide exercises

Doing the weekly exercises in this book benefits both you and the group. By completing them, as well as attending the meetings, you'll be able to get the most that you can out of DivorceCare. It also prepares you for the discussion time. Group discussions reach their full potential when everyone does the exercises.

## Don't date within the group

We do not allow dating among group members (or group leaders and group members) and strongly urge you to consider not dating at all while attending DivorceCare. This is a time for healing and building emotional strength. A new dating relationship more often than not distracts a person from the inner healing that needs to take place first. As a healthy alternative to dating, we encourage you to make friends with those of the same sex and exchange contact information to support each other during this time.

## Be respectful

Everyone in the group comes from different situations and backgrounds. Be respectful of the differences, knowing that group members are there to find hope, comfort, and healing. Also, make every effort to avoid speaking of others (including your former spouse) in disparaging or slanderous terms.

## Maintain confidentiality

Don't talk about things you hear in the group to people outside the group. This will help develop an atmosphere of trust. (But also keep in mind, there is no way the group can guarantee confidentiality, so use discretion about what you share.) A simple rule to remember—never tell someone else's story!

# THE FOUNDATION FOR *Healing*

## *A personal relationship with Jesus Christ*

Throughout DivorceCare you will hear people talking about the importance of a personal relationship with Jesus Christ in healing from divorce. In fact, you will hear it said that you cannot fully heal from divorce without the power of Christ in your life.

*Please read the information in this section carefully. It will show you how to have a personal relationship with Jesus Christ and how this relationship can make a real difference in your life.*

### What is at the center of my life?

You tend to "orbit" around certain people, things, or events in your life. They are the relationships, possessions, and circumstances you value most. They give meaning to life and bring joy to you.

Here are some examples:
> Job
> Children
> Husband or wife
> Financial resources
> Favorite activities
> Friends
> Health
> Houses, cars, and possessions

**Take a minute and list the people or things that your life revolves around. It may be one thing or a combination of items.**

_____

_____

_____

## How solid is my center?

In our solar system, planets have a predictable orbit because the sun is a stable gravitational "center." Imagine what would happen to those planets if the sun suddenly disappeared. **Now look at your list comprising the things at the center of your life. Which are permanent (cannot disappear or be lost)?**

Most things in your life can disappear. A husband or wife can leave the marriage or die. Your financial condition can suddenly change. Possessions break, rust, and wear out. Your health can deteriorate. When these things happen, you lose what you had been relying on for your stability. As a result, your "orbit" will destabilize, sending your life into an emotional tumble.

In the end, only one thing is permanent—a relationship with God. If you have one, it cannot be taken away. Because this relationship with God is so critical to your stability, it's important to know for sure that you have the kind of relationship with Him that will ensure He is permanently in the center of your life.

## Achieving permanent stability

How can God become the center of your life? The first step is to remove a major barrier between yourself and Him.

The Bible says that our sins separate us from having a relationship with God. When we put anything other than God at the center of our lives, this is sin. Picture this: You invite a friend over to talk about your problems. Your friend arrives, turns on the TV, and barely nods at you. Your friend then surfs the net for a while and motions "not yet" when you ask for a minute of time. After that, your friend prepares one sandwich and munches on it while catching up on phone calls. While it's certainly not wrong for your friend to watch TV, use the phone and internet, and eat, it's hurtful that your friend centered on everything but you. How much more do you think God disapproves of us when we prioritize and value the things He's created for us to enjoy more than we value Him?

In addition to possessions, time, and activities, we might put money, worries about the future, and even our family first in our lives before God. Other sins are more easily recognizable: bitterness, gossip, fits of rage, lies, judging others, not taking responsibility for our wrongs, desiring revenge, and sexual immorality.

Romans 3:23 says, **"For all have sinned and fall short of the glory of God."** The book of Romans also says that the result of sin is death (separation from God). **"For the wages of sin is death, but the gift of God is eternal life in Christ Jesus our Lord."** (Romans 6:23)

Your sin keeps you from God. Many people try to "earn" a relationship with Him by "being a good person" and "doing good things." But notice in the previous verse (Romans 6:23) that eternal life is a gift. It cannot be earned. You must receive it from the Giver.

**"For it is by grace you have been saved, through faith—and this is not from yourselves, it is the gift of God—not by works, so that no one can boast."** (Ephesians 2:8–9)

## Breaking through the barrier

If you can't overcome your sin and earn a relationship with God, how can He become the center of your life? The Bible says that Jesus Christ removed the barrier between God and you by dying in your place. He paid the price for your disobedience. Romans 5:8 puts it this way: **"But God demonstrates his own love for us in this: While we were still sinners, Christ died for us."** It's also important to realize that Jesus Christ is the only way to a relationship with God. John 14:6 reads, **"Jesus answered, 'I am the way and the truth and the life. No one comes to the Father except through me.'"**

## Making it real in my life

Maybe right now you ache for the stability, security, and wholeness that come from having God at the center of your life. Once He's there, you can access His power to help you heal from your separation or divorce. He can help stabilize your life's orbit.

The first step is to believe that Jesus is God's only Son and that He died to pay the price for your sins (the things you have done wrong). **"God made him who had no sin to be sin for us, so that in him we might become the righteousness of God."** (2 Corinthians 5:21) After believing this, you need to turn control of your life over to Jesus. In effect, He becomes the center of your life.

## How can God become the center of my life?

The Bible says that each person must surrender to Jesus as personal Lord and Savior through faith. To do this, you must first realize that you are a sinner and repent of (turn away from) your sin. The Bible says, **"Repent, then, and turn to God, so that your sins may be wiped out, that times of refreshing may come from the Lord."** (Acts 3:19)

Receiving Jesus through faith means trusting Him alone as the payment for your sin and surrendering your life to Him. **"If you declare with your mouth, 'Jesus is Lord,' and believe in your heart that God raised him from the dead, you will be saved. For it is with your heart that you believe and are justified, and it is with your mouth that you profess your faith and are saved."** (Romans 10:9–10)

## Taking the step

If you would like to surrender your life to Jesus Christ, here is a prayer you can pray. Why not do it right now?

*Dear God, I know I have done things that are wrong. Please forgive me for these sins. I turn control of my life over to Jesus, Your Son. I want Him to be my Savior and Lord. As my Savior, I rely on Him to save me from the effect of my sins through His death on the cross. As my Lord, I put Jesus at the center of my life and give Him control of it. Thank you for forgiving my sin and giving me the gift of eternal life with You. In Jesus' name I pray. Amen.*

**If that prayer expresses the desire of your heart, your relationship with God through Jesus Christ can never be taken from you:**

"My sheep listen to my voice; I know them, and they follow me. I give them eternal life, and they shall never perish; no one will snatch them out of my hand. My Father, who has given them to me, is greater than all; no one can snatch them out of my Father's hand." (John 10:27–29)

## 8 things that are really different now

If you invited Christ into your life, many things have changed. Look at what has happened.

1. **CHRIST IS IN YOUR LIFE:** *"And this is the testimony: God has given us eternal life, and this life is in his Son. Whoever has the Son has life; whoever does not have the Son of God does not have life. I write these things to you who believe in the name of the Son of God so that you may know that you have eternal life."* (1 John 5:11–13)

2. **CHRIST'S POWER IS IN YOUR LIFE:** *"I can do all this through him who gives me strength."* (Philippians 4:13)

3. **YOUR SINS WERE FORGIVEN:** *"In him we have redemption through his blood, the forgiveness of sins, in accordance with the riches of God's grace."* (Ephesians 1:7)

4. **YOU BECAME A PERMANENT PART OF GOD'S KINGDOM:** *"Therefore, since we are receiving a kingdom that cannot be shaken, let us be thankful, and so worship God acceptably with reverence and awe."* (Hebrews 12:28)

5. **YOU RECEIVED THE GIFT OF ETERNAL LIFE:** *"For God so loved the world that he gave his one and only Son, that whoever believes in him shall not perish but have eternal life."* (John 3:16)

6. **YOU CAN FIND ABUNDANT LIFE NOW:** *"The thief comes only to steal and kill and destroy; I have come that they may have life, and have it to the full."* (John 10:10)

7. **YOU CAN FIND GOD'S PEACE:** *"Do not be anxious about anything, but in every situation, by prayer and petition, with thanksgiving, present your requests to God. And the peace of God, which transcends all understanding, will guard your hearts and your minds in Christ Jesus."* (Philippians 4:6–7)

8. **GOD'S SPIRIT LIVES IN YOU:** *"And I will ask the Father, and he will give you another advocate to help you and be with you forever—the Spirit of truth. The world cannot accept him, because it neither sees him nor knows him. But you know him, for he lives with you and will be in you."* (John 14:16–17)

## What's next?

If you have surrendered your life to Jesus, let your DivorceCare leader know. He or she can connect you with a pastor, counselor, or a mature Christian friend to help you grow.

A good way to learn more about Jesus Christ is to read the book of John, found in the New Testament of the Bible. We suggest you commit to reading a chapter of this exciting book each day. As you read, pray that you will gain an even better understanding of how Jesus is changing your life.

It's also important for you to spend time with people who can help you know Jesus in an even deeper and more intimate way. The best way to do this is to become part of a church that will teach you and guide you in a growing relationship with Jesus.

# Watch DivorceCare videos online—for free

## CATCH UP, GET AHEAD, OR REVIEW

**DIVORCECARE.ORG/MY**

## Access session videos online

You can watch the very same DivorceCare videos you see during DivorceCare meetings, in your home. It's a great way to:

- Catch up if you miss a meeting
- Watch a video before your session begins
- Review a video you've already seen

## And much more ...

See additional bonus videos from the previous editions of DivorceCare for free.

## How to watch?

**DIVORCECARE.ORG/MY**

### Need help? Talk to your DivorceCare leader!

# WHO'S IN THE VIDEOS?

Each week you'll watch a video that features practical advice, guidance, and encouragement from experts in divorce recovery fields and from people who've been through separation and divorce. Steve Grissom and Denise Hildreth Jones are your cohosts on this weekly journey.

## YOUR VIDEO COHOSTS

**STEVE GRISSOM**, founder and president of Church Initiative, knows firsthand the devastation of divorce. After experiencing healing from his own divorce, he followed God's calling over the years to create and produce a support group resource that churches could use to help people hurting from broken marriages. Steve remarried, and he and his wife, Cheryl, designed and developed the DivorceCare program. Today DivorceCare, as well as Church Initiative's other care group resources (GriefShare and DivorceCare for Kids), are found in thousands of churches worldwide.

**DENISE HILDRETH JONES**, author and speaker, is the founder of Reclaiming Hearts Ministries. After 13 years of marriage, Denise's painful journey through divorce brought her to a place of heartbreak, fear, and disappointment. God's healing from this hurt formed the basis of her book *Reclaiming Your Heart: A Journey Back to Laughing, Loving, and Living* and ignited her passion for helping others reclaim their hearts. Denise remarried, and she and her husband, Philly, now lead Reclaiming Hearts Ministries, offering Bible studies and events that challenge people to be transformed by God's Word.

## DIVORCECARE EXPERTS

You'll meet these people on the DivorceCare videos in the coming weeks. They are experts on divorce and recovery topics (some have experienced divorce themselves) and can help guide your recovery from the hurt of separation or divorce.

**DR. JOHN APPLEGATE** is a board-certified psychiatrist and director of the Christian counseling and psychiatry group practice John Applegate, MD & Associates. He serves as executive director of Philadelphia Renewal Network, a nonprofit organization that works with local churches to provide affordable counseling. **jaanda.com**

**KEITH BATTLE** is the senior pastor of Zion Church in Landover, MD. Since its start in 1999, Zion Church has grown from 25 to 5,000 regular attendees. His ministry is focused on helping people to experience God, engage in community, and be equipped and empowered for ministry.

 **SABRINA BLACK** is a counselor, speaker, author, professor, and life coach. She is president of the National Biblical Counselors Association, founding member of the American Association of Christian Counselors, and clinical director of Abundant Life Counseling Center in Detroit, MI. She is the author of more than 10 books and workbooks including *Live Right Now*. **abundantlifecounseling.webs.com**

 **ELSA KOK COLOPY** is a speaker and author. Her books include *Settling for Less Than God's Best?: A Relationship Checkup for Single Women*; *A Woman Who Hurts, A God Who Heals*; and *The Single Mom's Guide to Finding Joy in the Chaos*. A divorced single parent for 12 years, Elsa is now remarried and is the mother of eight. She continues to travel and speak. **elsakokcolopy.com**

 **RON L. DEAL** is a licensed marriage and family therapist with an expertise in blended families. He is founder of Smart Stepfamilies and director of FamilyLife Blended, and he's authored numerous works on stepfamily living, including the best-selling book *The Smart Stepfamily*. **smartstepfamilies.com**

 **DR. ERIKKA DZIRASA** is a board-certified adult, child, and adolescent psychiatrist. She specializes in anxiety disorders, mood disorders, trauma, and psychotic disorders. She has served as president of the North Carolina Council of Child & Adolescent Psychiatry and as a subject matter advisor for the nonprofit organization "I Live For."

 **DR. MIGUEL ECHEVARRIA** serves as director of Hispanic Leadership Development and assistant professor of New Testament and Greek at Southeastern Baptist Theological Seminary in Wake Forest, NC. A native of Miami, FL, he is married and has four daughters.

 **JOY FORREST** is founder and executive director of Called to Peace Ministries. After going through divorce herself, she now holds a master's degree in biblical counseling and is a certified advocate with the North Carolina Coalition Against Domestic Violence. She has worked with over 1,000 domestic abuse survivors and authored *Called to Peace*. **calledtopeace.org**

 **DR. BRAD HAMBRICK** has authored seven books, including *God's Attributes: Rest for Life's Struggles* and *Self-Centered Spouse: Help for Chronically Broken Marriages*. He is pastor of counseling at The Summit Church in North Carolina and serves as assistant professor of biblical counseling at Southeastern Baptist Theological Seminary. **bradhambrick.com**

 **DR. CRAIG KEENER** is an author whose publications include 25 books, seven booklets, and hundreds of articles. He is professor of New Testament at Asbury Theological Seminary in Kentucky and is on the executive committee of the Evangelical Theological Society. Dr. Keener has experienced divorce himself and knows firsthand the many struggles people face. **craigkeener.com**

 **OMAR KING** holds a master of divinity in biblical counseling and is a certified clinical pastoral educator. He serves as a full-time staff counselor at Bridgehaven Counseling Associates in North Carolina, where his areas of focus include issues related to marriage, premarriage, dating, depression, trauma, and abuse.

**TIFFANY LESNIK** is a licensed attorney in North Carolina with a master's degree in clinical psychology. After experiencing domestic violence in her former marriage, she now uses her experience to help others escape abuse and suffering, focusing her practice on cases involving domestic violence and high-conflict custody. **lesnik-law.com**

**DR. CRAWFORD LORITTS** is a world-renowned speaker and author. He is senior pastor of Fellowship Bible Church in Roswell, GA, and frequently travels for speaking engagements at conferences, sporting events, and colleges around the globe.

**TRAY & MELODY LOVVORN** are speakers and teachers on the subjects of marriage, parenting, sexual addiction, and betrayal trauma. After having been divorced themselves, they now provide life and marriage coaching, recovery intensives, and parenting solutions through their nonprofit Undone Redone. **undoneredone.com**

**LT. CHRIS MINOR** has 23 years of experience as a police officer, responding to a variety of calls that include domestic violence and divorce-related issues. He coordinates the Department Crisis Intervention Team, which assists people in crisis events.

**DR. LINDA MINTLE** has been in clinical practice as a licensed therapist for 30 years. As a best-selling author, she has written 20 books, including *I Married You, Not Your Family*. Known as "The Relationship Doctor," she is a national speaker and news consultant and hosts her own show on Faith Radio. **drlindamintle.com**

**DR. ELIAS MOITINHO** is professor of counseling at Liberty University in Virginia. He has years of experience serving as a pastor, counselor, professor, and the director of a Christian counseling center. His website provides videos and instructional articles for personal growth in life, marriage, and family. **motivationandgrowth.com**

**DR. TIM MUEHLHOFF** is professor of communication studies at Biola University, where he also serves as director of resources for Biola's Center for Marriage and Relationships. His Neighbor Love initiative provides marital resources at no cost to low-income communities, and his podcast, *The Art of Relationships*, is heard in over 70 countries. **timmuehlhoff.com**

**DR. RAMON PRESSON** is a licensed marriage and family therapist in Tennessee. He is founder of The Marriage Counseling Center of Franklin, located just outside of Nashville. A weekly newspaper columnist, he has also authored several books, including *When Will My Life Not Suck?: Authentic Hope for the Disillusioned*. **ramonpressontherapy.com**

**DAVE RAMSEY** is a personal money-management expert and a national radio personality. He has authored several books, including *Financial Peace* and *The Total Money Makeover*. He is the creator of Financial Peace University, a program that helps people get rid of debt and manage their money. **daveramsey.com**

**VANEETHA RISNER** is an author and speaker who shares how she has found hope through her challenges with polio, the loss of a son, and an unwanted divorce. Her books include *The Scars That Have Shaped Me* and *Walking Through Fire*. **vaneetha.com**

**KEN SANDE** is president of Relational Wisdom 360 and founder of Peacemaker Ministries. He teaches internationally and is the author of numerous books and training resources, including *The Peacemaker* and *Resolving Everyday Conflict*. **rw360.org**

**TRAVIS SASSER** is a board-certified consumer bankruptcy attorney in North Carolina. A graduate of the University of Georgia School of Law, he frequently represents debtors who are struggling to work through the financial aftermath of separation and divorce. **sasserbankruptcy.com**

**GEORGIA SHAFFER** is a professional certified coach and licensed psychologist in Pennsylvania. Georgia went through the loss of her marriage and her job. After those experiences, she wrote *Taking Out Your Emotional Trash* and *A Gift of Mourning Glories*, which provide personal guidance for rebuilding after loss. **georgiashaffer.com**

**LESLIE VERNICK** is a licensed clinical social worker, national speaker, and relationship coach with expertise in marriage improvement and conflict resolution. Her books include *The Emotionally Destructive Marriage and How to Live Right When Your Life Goes Wrong*. **leslievernick.com**

**DR. STEPHEN VIARS** is pastor of Faith Church and a counselor at Faith Biblical Counseling Ministries in Lafayette, IN. He speaks at conferences, colleges, and seminaries in the US and abroad. He authored *Putting Your Past in Its Place: Moving Forward in Freedom and Forgiveness*.

**SGT. A. J. WISNIEWSKI, RET.**, served on the Raleigh, NC, police force for 27 years. He has experience in sexual assault investigations, SWAT, and a year with the FBI for violent crimes. He also worked five years as a 911 dispatcher, taking calls for incidents related to domestic disputes and family violence, as well as problems associated with drugs, alcohol, and other crime-related issues.

# PERSONAL STORIES

These people tell their stories in the videos and participant guide. Here's some background information they shared with us to help you get to know them better:

**ALISA** has five kids and seven grandkids, and loves to sing. She told us how her life was turned upside down by an unexpected divorce, leaving her feeling hurt and abandoned. Through this experience, she is learning about herself, God, and the importance of being connected to friends and family.

**ALLEN** is a history buff who enjoys cooking and travel. He explained that when their only son left for college, he and his wife realized they had been drifting apart for years and decided to separate. Through DivorceCare, Allen discovered new meaning in life as a single person after his divorce.

**ANNETTE** is a property field adjuster and mom of three. She shared with us how after 10 years of marriage, she was blindsided by divorce papers following the discovery that her husband was having an affair. Annette joined a DivorceCare group where she found hope and healing and is now content in her new life.

**CAROL** is a retired teacher and former foreign service officer. After 28 years of marriage and the birth of two children, she and her husband agreed to an amicable divorce. They have worked to maintain an ongoing friendship for the sake of their family.

**CHE-VON** is a mom of three and an elementary school principal who enjoys reading, walking, and African-American history. Che-Von shared in her interview how 12 years after marrying her high school sweetheart, she decided to divorce, due to her husband's infidelity and lack of emotional and financial support.

**CHUCK** shared how he had been married for almost five years when his former wife revealed that she no longer loved him and wanted a divorce. After a season mixed with anger, grief, and guilt, Chuck is now remarried, and he serves in his church by helping others who are experiencing divorce, single parenting, and becoming a blended family.

**CONNIE** has been married to her second husband, Dan, for 23 years and has two adult daughters. Connie disclosed that her first marriage ended after she discovered her husband was having an inappropriate relationship with one of their foster daughters. She found hope and healing by participating in a DivorceCare group and is now a DivorceCare leader.

**DETRICK** became a DivorceCare leader after a life-changing experience as a DivorceCare participant. He received incredible support after his wife told him she wanted a divorce, and now Detrick wants to give back and help others in the same way.

**DOUG** is a father of four and enjoys coaching and public speaking. He shared with us how after 20 years of marriage, his wife moved out of the bedroom, blaming it on snoring. A two-year separation followed, and then they divorced. Still in love with his wife, Doug has struggled to accept that she does not share his feelings, to the point that it initially affected his health.

**JONATHON** is a school teaching assistant and pro wrestling enthusiast. He's a hands-on single dad and enjoys participating in martial arts with his four children. In his interview, Jonathon explained how 14 years into their marriage, his wife left him for another woman. Since then, he has found strong support from friends and family as he shoulders his parenting responsibilities.

**KATHY** is director of ministry coaching at Church Initiative. Kathy shared in her interview that her husband of 15 years had been unfaithful with multiple women, and after many attempts to make the marriage work, she eventually sought a divorce. She's been married to her second husband for 16 years and feels blessed to use her experience in helping others through DivorceCare.

**KIMBERLY** and her ex-husband dated through high school and college and eventually married. They were best friends until alcoholism entered the picture. Kimberly talked about how her husband's drinking destroyed their finances and ultimately their marriage. She also shared how DivorceCare helped her confront her own part in the marital breakdown and deal with her anger.

**MARY LOU** shared in her interview how her marriage ended primarily due to the consequences of her husband's alcohol abuse. She is using her experience to help others as a support group facilitator at her home church and as a women's small-group leader. Post-divorce, she has continued her work as a dental hygienist and finds enjoyment in art and dancing.

**MIKE** is an engineer with a special interest in gardening. He was happily married for 24 years, when he came home from work one day to find the house cleaned out and his wife gone. Mike shared that her explanation was "I want my freedom."

**QUIN** is a reservation agent who loves to travel, sew, and do volunteer work. After 33 years of marriage, her husband left her and their five children and pursued divorce.

**RICHARD** is a firefighter and EMT who loves to fish, read, and spend time with his two dogs. Eight years ago, Richard and his wife divorced. Since then, Richard and his ex-wife have forgiven each other for the hurts surrounding the divorce and are working on a civil relationship.

**SALLY** is a mother of three and enjoys her work with young children. Sally thought she and her husband had the perfect life together, until her husband's mother died. After this, he asked for a divorce. While still in denial that the divorce was actually happening, Sally discovered DivorceCare, where she learned principles that have given her hope about her future.

**TERRY** is a self-employed architect and engineer who enjoys long-distance bicycle touring. He married his first girlfriend and soon discovered they did not communicate effectively. The lack of communication led to separate lives and a lot of silence. Terry shared with us how after 20 years of marriage, he was blindsided by divorce when his wife suddenly left and didn't tell him until she was on a plane heading overseas.

**THERESA** was married for three years when her husband left her for another woman. She shared that he cut off all communication and financial support, abandoning her and their two children. During the divorce process, Theresa found incredible support from her friends, and she now credits her faith for carrying her through and bringing beauty from the ashes of divorce.

**VICKILYNN** is a retired mom and grandma, cookbook writer, and blogger. Vickilynn explained how after 35 years of marriage, she discovered there had been repeated incidents of infidelity. When it became evident that restoration was not possible after two years of separation, she and her husband divorced. Now she helps women deal with the pain of divorce through DivorceCare.

# DEEP *Hurt*

## *The surprising effects of divorce*

You never realized you could feel this many emotions at once—or that your mind could go in so many directions. You may be wondering how you're going to handle it all.

This week's **video**, **On My Own** exercises, and **My Weekly Journal** will help you sort through the chaos in your mind and start taking steps toward healing and finding hope. You'll learn:

- **That overwhelming emotions and confusion are normal**
- **Healthy practices to set you up for a successful recovery**
- **How God can help you in your recovery process**

# VIDEO OUTLINE

Use this outline to write down important concepts, encouraging words, or questions you may have while viewing the video.

## THE DEVASTATION

## REBUILDING TAKES TIME

Because divorce is

- Long, complicated, and invasive
- Disorienting and confusing
- Emotionally overwhelming

## REBUILDING TAKES PLANNING

Monitor your eating habits

Ask wise, trustworthy friends to help you

Turn to God in prayer

Consider other sources of support

# HOW DIVORCECARE CAN HELP

## Additional help

# ON MY *Own*

## Wisdom and encouragement for your new journey

### THERESA'S STORY

*"Once the divorce papers were filed, I thought,* What's going to happen to me? What is going to happen to my children? *It was as if somebody had come in and taken a hammer to my life. My life was in shards on the ground, and what do I pick up first? It's also like you're falling off this cliff and you don't know when you're going to land, how hard you're going to land, or if you're going to be okay when you land."* You might feel a lot like Theresa, tumbling over that cliff. This week, you'll receive practical tools and insights to help you with the challenges you're facing.

## 1 HAS ANYONE ELSE EVER FELT LIKE THIS?

It might feel like your emotions are "off the scale," but what you're experiencing is actually pretty normal. It's also common to have trouble expressing what you're going through.

That's one reason God gave us the Psalms in the Bible. Thousands of years ago, many of the people who wrote these words were experiencing deep emotional pain. And you can use their words to pray and cry out to God today.

### GOD'S MESSAGE TO YOU

*"1 Save me, O God, for the waters have come up to my neck. 2 I sink in the miry depths, where there is no foothold. I have come into the deep waters; the floods engulf me. 3 I am worn out calling for help."* (Psalm 69:1–3a)

*"2 How long must I wrestle with my thoughts and day after day have sorrow in my heart? How long will my enemy triumph over me? … 5 But I trust in your [God's] unfailing love; my heart rejoices in your salvation."* (Psalm 13:2, 5)

1. **Circle the parts of today's verses you can most relate to.**

2. **Where do you usually turn when your emotions become overwhelming?**
   (Check all that apply.)

   ☒ Family or friends

   ☐ Television or web surfing

   ☐ Substances or food

   ☐ God/the Bible

   ☐ Other _____

3. David (who wrote these psalms) says his difficulty is like drowning! Who is his "life-guard"? Why does David call out to Him?

## REMEMBER

- You aren't the first (or last) to experience the emotions you're feeling.

- God has provided the Psalms to help you express your sorrows, hopes, and regrets to Him.

*"I felt embarrassed. And I was angry. Very angry."*
– Richard

2
## SCATTERED BRAIN? HOW TO STAY ON TASK

When you're in a marriage breakup, you're trying to navigate unfamiliar terrain—and you may not even know which way is north! It might be hard to keep your tasks, activities, and responsibilities from swirling chaotically in your mind.

To organize your thoughts and stay on task, try these four tips:

1. **Write it down:** You can't expect yourself to re-member everything, so it helps just to get things out of your mind. Writing a to-do list relieves some of the stress because you no longer have to try to remember everything. Whew!

2. **Tackle tasks, not projects:** Sometimes you can get bogged down because you put projects on your to-do list instead of tasks. Projects are actually multiple tasks, which need to be broken down into smaller, more manageable tasks. For instance, instead of "Clean my closet," break it down into "Sort my shoes," "Pull out shirts I haven't worn in six months," etc.

3. **Prioritize by importance:** Sometimes things that are urgent keep us from doing the things that are important. Schedule time to do things that will benefit you long term, like exercising, preparing healthy meals, spending time with children, and praying.

4. **Chart your to-do list:** It can help to put all your to-dos in a chart based on when you need to do them—today, this month, etc. Also include the resources you'll need to get them done (money, supplies, a babysitter). Download a free chart at **divorcecare.org/my**. Consider sharing your chart with friends who want to help, but don't know how.

*"Just to get out of bed was a feat in itself."* – Theresa

3
## FEELING STRESSED? TRY CHANGING YOUR MENU

Separation and divorce take a toll on your mind and body. You probably feel run-down both mentally and physically. Unfortunately, when you're stressed, it's tempting to ignore what your body needs to stay strong. And when you do that, your body isn't able to overcome the stress.

Throughout this book, you'll find tips that will help you maintain your physical health while dealing with your separation or divorce.

The chart below shows the food your body—especially your brain!—needs to function well. And any diet that promotes good heart and digestive health is also associated with less anxiety and depression over time.

To keep both mind and body in good health, try making these adjustments:[1]

| Eat MORE of these | Eat LESS of these |
| --- | --- |
| Colorful fruits and vegetables (dark green, red, orange, yellow), 2–3 cups a day | Refined sugar (as in ice cream, baked goods, candy) |
| Whole grains (including brown rice), 3 or more ounces a day | Refined flour (as in baked goods, pastas), white rice |
| Lean sources of protein: fish, seafood, yogurt, skinless chicken, 5–6 ounces a day | Beef, pork, processed meats |
| Canola, safflower, sunflower, or olive oil, up to 2 tablespoons a day | Highly saturated fats (animal fats, butter, coconut oil, palm kernel oil) |
| Seeds and nuts, about an ounce a day | Potatoes |
| Skim or low-fat (1%) dairy products (milk, yogurt, cheese), about 3 cups a day | Whole-dairy products |

*"It's hard when you're cooking for one."* – Carol

## 4 WHERE CAN I FEEL SAFE?

It's even more painful when you're hurt by someone you love—when a person who's supposed to protect you is the one you need protection from. It's in these heartbreaking moments that you need a perfect, loving Protector.

## GOD'S MESSAGE TO YOU

*"1 LORD, how many are my foes! How many rise up against me! 2 Many are saying of me, 'God will not deliver him.' 3 But you, LORD, are a shield around me, my glory, the One who lifts my head high."* (Psalm 3:1–3)

*"Give your burdens to the LORD, and he will take care of you."* (Psalm 55:22a NLT)

1. **According to these verses, what will God do for you when people who want to hurt you come against you?**

2. **What burdens are you currently carrying? What does Psalm 55:22 say to do with those burdens?**

## REMEMBER

- God hears you when you cry out to Him.

- When you need protection, God is the strongest shield you could ever hold on to.

*"It's like you're walking through a war zone."* – Theresa

## 5 I NEED BACKUP!

The road ahead looks hard. You see hazards, and you're pretty sure more hurts are around the next bend. Maybe you wonder how you're going to survive this journey.

David, who wrote many of the psalms, had some of the same thoughts. He was betrayed, was pursued by enemies, and fought many physical, emotional, and spiritual battles. How did he handle all of this? He had some help.

# GOD'S MESSAGE TO YOU

"*6 Praise be to the LORD, for he has heard my cry for mercy. 7 The LORD is my strength and my shield; my heart trusts in him, and he helps me. My heart leaps for joy, and with my song I praise him.*" (Psalm 28:6–7)

"*3 Since you [God] are my rock and my fortress, for the sake of your name lead and guide me. 4 Keep me free from the trap that is set for me, for you are my refuge. 5 Into your hands I commit my spirit; deliver me, LORD, my faithful God.*" (Psalm 31:3–5)

1. **According to today's verses, where did David turn when he needed help?**

2. **What words are used to describe God in these verses? Based on these descriptions, how can God help you?**

**BRIGHTER DAYS**

## THERESA'S STORY

"*When I look back at what has happened in just a year and a half, I think, How in the world did I get through that? I still have days where that wave of sadness crashes over me. But I can tell you that I don't cry as often, and I find joy in doing things I used to enjoy.*

"*It's not the end. And if you take time to enjoy the small things, whether it's cooking, another hobby, talking with a friend, or going for a walk—something very minor can be major in your recovery. I still have a long way to go, but I don't feel hopeless, or helpless, or have that fear like it's never going to end.*"

# REMEMBER

- You're never alone in your struggles—you can always ask God for help.

- As your rock, fortress, shield, and strength, God can handle any problems you face.

- When you begin to trust God, you may not have the same emotional reaction that David did. But as your understanding of God deepens, you'll experience more peace and joy when you turn your problems over to Him.

## NEXT SESSION

How to avoid the roadblocks to your recovery.

# MY WEEKLY Journal

As you go through the trauma of separation or divorce, you'll experience a whirlwind of thoughts and emotions. Confusion is common—it can be hard to make sense of it all!

But there is something you can do to help calm the inner storm: journal. This practice can be extremely beneficial. First, it can slow ... down ... your ... racing ... mind. Second, writing about your experiences can help you think more clearly about them, which is critical for solving problems. Third, your journal also becomes a record of progress and growth as you move forward with recovery.

We recommend making a journal entry each day. Ultimately it's best to allow 15 minutes to do this. But as you're getting started, aim for 5 minutes and gradually spend more time journaling. You can use a spiral notebook or a digital recorder. Be sure to include the date of the entries. And remember, you don't need to share this with anyone, so be honest in your entries.

This week, start journaling by completing the following statements:

1.  **Today, I struggled with ... and I felt ...**

2.  **Today, I felt a little better when ...**

## CHART YOUR PROGRESS

Place a check in the boxes to identify how you are feeling in each area this week: emotionally, physically, etc. Even better? Substitute a word or two to describe how you are doing.

|  | REALLY BAD | OKAY | PRETTY GOOD | GREAT |
|---|---|---|---|---|
| **Emotionally** |  |  |  |  |
| **Physically** |  |  |  |  |
| **Spiritually** (closeness to God) |  |  |  |  |
| **Relationally** (closeness to others) |  |  |  |  |
| **How your life is in general** |  |  |  |  |

# FOR Parents

## How to tell your kids about the divorce

When telling the children about an upcoming divorce, a lot depends upon your situation, the age of the children, and your family dynamics. You may be wondering where to start, what to include, how to explain things.

### What to say

It is best if both parents come together to tell the children about the divorce. Find a place that is comfortable and with no distractions.

Start the conversation by telling your children how much you love them. Keep the conversation basic and reassuring. You might start by saying something like: "Mom [Dad] and I have been having some adult problems. We are going to be separating and getting a divorce. We both love you so very much. And none of this is your fault."

Be up-front and honest when talking to the children. Speak slowly and distinctly so the children can grasp what is being said.

Sometimes the cause of a breakup is primarily due to the behavior of one spouse (e.g., an affair, abuse, addictions); it can be difficult to know what to tell the kids. Give children basic, age-appropriate information. Say something like: "When people do or say very harmful things, you may need to change the relationship. Your Mommy [Daddy] made some choices that were not very nice. So we needed to change the relationship. We can still pray for her, and you can still love her."

### How to say it

- **Young children**

  **Define it:** Tell them what divorce means. ("This means I'm going to live here with you, and Mom [Dad] is going to live in another place. You're going to spend time in both places.")

**Explain it:** Be specific about how it affects their life. Tell them what will stay the same and what will be different. ("You'll still go to the same school, but we won't all live in the same house.")

- **Elementary school children**

  **Explain at their level:** At this age, kids need less information about what divorce is, but they still need to understand how divorce will affect them. And if they've heard rumors, they will need you to be truthful and answer each question as best you can without bashing their other parent.

- **Teenagers**

  **Tell, ask, listen:** Teens bring their own ideas about divorce to the table. After telling them about the divorce, ask them what they think about it. Offer facts (calmly and without judgment) as best you can.

### When to say it

After they hear this news, your kids will need the reassurance of your presence. Therefore, be wise about the timing of the conversation. For instance, don't tell them you're getting a divorce, and then go on a business trip the next day.

### How to respond

- **Let them react:** Don't try to squash their reactions. Offer empathy and support. You want your children to know they have the freedom to talk and ask questions. Help them feel safe when they talk with you.

- **Reassure them:** Tell the children again how much you love them and that it's not their fault. Young kids in particular assume they did something that caused this. Tell them over and over that it's not their fault and you love them.

# Watch DivorceCare videos online—for free

## CATCH UP, GET AHEAD, OR REVIEW

**DIVORCECARE.ORG/MY**

## Access session videos online

You can watch the very same DivorceCare videos you see during DivorceCare meetings, in your home. It's a great way to:

- Catch up if you miss a meeting
- Watch a video before your session begins
- Review a video you've already seen

## And much more ...

See additional bonus videos from the previous editions of DivorceCare for free.

## How to watch?

**DIVORCECARE.ORG/MY**

**Need help? Talk to your DivorceCare leader!**

# ROAD TO *Recovery*

*Finding and following the path to healing*

Am I headed in the right direction? Which way is up? Where do I turn?

The road ahead looks really rough—how can I make it through?

This week's **video**, **On My Own** exercises, and **My Weekly Journal** will help you answer these questions, as you learn:

- **Common roadblocks to recovery from divorce**
- **Possible "mile markers" of progress in your recovery**
- **Why trusting God in your recovery is a practical choice**

## VIDEO OUTLINE

Use this outline to write down important concepts, encouraging words, or questions you may have while viewing the video.

## ROADBLOCKS ALONG THE WAY

Numbing the pain

- Alcohol
- Drugs
- Work
- Spending
- Internet
- Gaming

Premature relationships

Tend to be more about

- Rescue
- Filling a role
- Selfish validation

Isolation

Focusing on guilt and shame

# SIGNPOSTS OF PROGRESS

You're not obsessing over your former spouse

- You're okay with his or her success
- You stop comparing the person
- You can be upset about other things
- You're not trolling social media
- You no longer have marital expectations

You see positive changes in your emotions

- Fewer negative emotion cycles
- More able to express freely
- Less prone to anger
- More positive sense of humor

You set healthy boundaries

You have a new outlook on the future

You are content with yourself

You are growing closer to God

- Talking to God in prayer
- Going back to church
- Recognizing God in everyday life
- Trusting God with the future

## Additional help

**Quin's story** —— pp. 14, 17

**My head is spinning** —— p. 15

**Who will heal my broken heart?** —— p. 16

# ON MY *Own*

## Wisdom and encouragement for your new journey

### QUIN'S STORY

*"When I was told he was leaving, I couldn't accept it. I was in denial. I was not willing to let him go. I was going to fight to the very end with every fiber of my being to save my marriage. I contested the divorce twice, to allow him time to really think about all he was forfeiting with the divorce. I would constantly try to find a way to stop him from making this decision. But the third time he finally won it. I was devastated."* Where do you go from here? This week, you'll discover some of the same truths Quin did, which provide direction for recovery after divorce or separation.

---

## 1 I HAVE NOWHERE TO TURN

When there are so many broken pieces to pick up, it's hard to know where to begin. Daily tasks can feel harder, especially when you're feeling alone in it all. It might be tempting to try to ignore or run away from the mess—or maybe your response is to dive in on your own and just hope you don't drown. But there is a third option.

### GOD'S MESSAGE TO YOU

*"**1** Truly my soul finds rest in God; my salvation comes from him. **2** Truly he is my rock and my salvation; he is my fortress, I will never be shaken."* (Psalm 62:1–2)

*"The name of the LORD is a fortified tower; the righteous run to it and are safe."* (Proverbs 18:10)

---

1. **As you face current stresses, check the boxes that describe your typical responses:**

   ☐ Overwhelmed

   ☐ Indecisive

   ☐ Doing anything possible to relieve or avoid stress

   ☐ Trying to handle everything on my own

   ☐ Finding rest and security in God

2. **The people who wrote today's Bible verses discovered that during stressful situations, they could find security and rest in God. List the words they use to describe God. What do these word-pictures tell you about God?**

3. If you thought of God in these terms, how would it affect your typical responses to stress?

## REMEMBER

- You're not facing your struggles alone. God wants you to run to Him. He can provide solid ground to stand on and strength to move forward.

- Deepening your understanding of who God is and His commitment to you results in calm confidence and trust.

*"I can't understand God as my rock unless I'm willing to acknowledge I'm feeling overwhelmed."*
– Dr. Stephen Viars

## IS GOD REALLY HERE? AND HELPING ME?

This God who loves you, bandages your wounds, and speaks truth into your life is a God who never leaves your side. Maybe you're thinking, *Is God really here? Do I really believe He's with me, supporting me and helping me every moment of the day?*

"I'm right here," says God.

## GOD'S MESSAGE TO YOU

*"The LORD replied, 'My Presence will go with you, and I will give you rest.'"* (Exodus 33:14)

*"You [God] will keep in perfect peace all who trust in you, all whose thoughts are fixed on you!"* (Isaiah 26:3 NLT)

*"8 If I go up to the heavens, you [God] are there; if I make my bed in the depths, you are there. 9 If I rise on the wings of the dawn, if I settle on the far side of the sea, 10 even there your hand will guide me, your right hand will hold me fast."* (Psalm 139:8–10)

1. According to Exodus 33 and Isaiah 26, how do you find rest and peace?

2. According to today's verses, if you make a wrong choice or go down a wrong path, where is God in relation to you?

3. No matter where you are, or what you're doing in a given moment, what will God do for you (see Psalm 139:10)?

## REMEMBER

- God gives you five words that can change your life if you really believe and live as if they are true, says Leslie Vernick: "I am with you always."

- Having a relationship with Jesus is the way to have God's presence in your life (see page ix).

## MY HEAD IS SPINNING

So many decisions to make. And little time or energy to think about them. It can feel overwhelming, even paralyzing. You're dealing with I-never-thought-I'd-be-here challenges. You're figuring out how to relate to people who knew you as part of a couple. You've got decisions to make about finances, kids, and your overloaded schedule.

You're probably thinking, *I could use a little help here!*

## GOD'S MESSAGE TO YOU

*"For the LORD gives wisdom; from his mouth come knowledge and understanding."* (Proverbs 2:6)

"*5 Trust in the LORD with all your heart and lean not on your own understanding; 6 in all your ways submit to him, and he will make your paths straight.*" (Proverbs 3:5–6)

"*Plans fail for lack of counsel, but with many advisers they succeed.*" (Proverbs 15:22)

1. **Name two decisions you're trying to make. What are some questions you have about these decisions?**

2. **If you were to trust God to help with your decisions, what would be the results, according to today's verses?**

3. **God brings people into our lives who have more experience or knowledge than we do. Whom could you ask for advice?** *(Note: If they don't know the Bible well or have a close relationship with God, run their advice past someone who does.)*

## REMEMBER

- God is the source of all wisdom, and He wants to help you by directing your path.

- God's wisdom and guidance are available in the Bible. The exercises and articles in this book will help you discover what God has to say and connect it with your life.

"*You need to slow everything down in your life.*"
– Sabrina Black

---

## 4  WHO WILL HEAL MY BROKEN HEART?

If you feel as if your heart is broken, don't lose hope, because you can be cared for, mended, and healed.

## GOD'S MESSAGE TO YOU

"*1 The LORD has anointed me [Jesus] to proclaim good news to the poor. He has sent me to bind up the broken-hearted, 2 … to comfort all who mourn, 3 and provide for those who grieve in Zion—to bestow on them a crown of beauty instead of ashes, the oil of joy instead of mourning, and a garment of praise instead of a spirit of despair.*" (Isaiah 61:1b–3a)

1. **List the words from these verses that best describe how you feel now.**

2. **The words "bind up" in today's verses literally mean "to bandage, to care for a wound." This is a powerful picture of God's care for you. List the words and images in today's Bible verses that describe how you would like to feel.**

3. **Use this space to tell God what you're thinking about your heartache and your desire for help. (Talk to God like you'd talk to a friend. Remember, He cares, and He can walk alongside you and bring healing.)**
   God, here's what I'm thinking …

## REMEMBER

- With God there is healing for anything—even the trauma of a marriage breakup.

- "An intimate relationship with God has meant joy in the midst of hardship, comfort in the midst of pain—real comfort, not the false stuff. It has meant contentment with life. A relationship with Him changes everything."
  – Elsa Kok Colopy

*"Nothing in God's economy is beyond repair. God does His best work with broken pieces."*
– Dr. Linda Mintle

## 5 DO WHATEVER I WANT, OR OBEY GOD?

Does it bother you that many people who ignore God appear to be happy and successful, without a care in the world? It might cause you to question your own choices.

Perhaps you're wondering why you shouldn't cast off restraints and just enjoy the "good life." If that's the case, you probably relate to Asaph, the man who wrote Psalm 73. He struggled to understand why people who rebelled against God seemed to prosper.

## GOD'S MESSAGE TO YOU

*"3 For I envied the arrogant when I saw the prosperity of the wicked. 4 They have no struggles; their bodies are healthy and strong. 12 … always free of care, they go on amassing wealth. 16 When I tried to understand all this, it troubled me deeply 17 till I entered the sanctuary of God; then I understood their final destiny. … 27 Those who are far from you will perish; you destroy all who are unfaithful to you. 28 But as for me, it is good to be near God. I have made the Sovereign LORD my refuge."*
(Psalm 73:3–4, 12b, 16–17, 27–28a)

1. **Do you ever envy others who seem to live a carefree life? Whom do you envy, and why? How has this affected your life?**

2. **What did Asaph conclude about the carefree life? What changed his perspective?**

## REMEMBER

- Choosing to stay near God ultimately results in peace, security, and contentment.

- Always consider the bigger picture as you make daily choices.

### QUIN'S STORY

*"Three things have been key in moving me forward with my life: reading the Bible, listening to music, and exercising. These have been major components in maintaining my strength and stability: mentally, emotionally, physically, and spiritually. [Reading] the Word of God gave me strength. It helped me to lay aside my fears and my doubts. I don't have to worry about what people are saying and what people think, because I have God's truth [that He is with me and will take care of me]. There was just this peace about it."*

## NEXT SESSION

Learn what to do with
your anger.

# MY WEEKLY Journal

Are you having trouble processing all the thoughts in your head? Is your brain on overload? It will help to get some of those thoughts out into your journal. You can use these prompts as a guide.

**1. This week, it was hardest when ...**

**2. When that happened, I ...**

**3. This went well because ... Or, it could have gone better if I ...**

**4. Something I learned from the video and On My Own exercises that could help with this is ...**

## CHART YOUR PROGRESS

Place a check in the boxes to identify how you are feeling in each area this week: emotionally, physically, etc. Even better? Substitute a word or two to describe how you are doing.

|  | REALLY BAD | OKAY | PRETTY GOOD | GREAT |
|---|---|---|---|---|
| **Emotionally** |  |  |  |  |
| **Physically** |  |  |  |  |
| **Spiritually** (closeness to God) |  |  |  |  |
| **Relationally** (closeness to others) |  |  |  |  |
| **How your life is in general** |  |  |  |  |

---

### *Are my kids okay?*

---

Children have a lot of adjusting to do after a divorce or separation. Your kids may look like they're recovering well, or you may notice they're struggling. But how can you really tell what's going on with them?

First understand that several factors affect how well your kids will handle the stresses of a family breakup:

- Their developmental age

- Their chronological age at the time of the divorce

- The parent relationship—is it cooperative, warring, indifferent?

- Their support system-–for the children and the entire family

- Their visitation schedules

- The introduction of a parent's new love interest

## Identifying roadblocks and milestones

As you monitor your children's recovery process, keep your eyes open for roadblocks that could be holding them back, as well as indicators that they've reached a new milestone in their recovery. Here are three ways to do that.

**Look for recurrent behaviors:** Many children experience anger and denial. These behaviors can indicate there are roadblocks keeping them from moving forward in healing.

- **Anger:** If they're angry, they may have difficulty sitting still or participating in normal activities.

- **Denial:** If they are in denial, they may refuse to do things that would force them to admit Mom and Dad are no longer together. If a child is in denial about the breakup, introducing a new love interest for either parent can be particularly challenging.

**Get input from others:** Check in with others who interact with your children to see what they have noticed about your children's behavior. Ask them to give you updates if they notice any progress or struggles in your children's attitude and actions. Good sources may include:

- Pastors

- Children's ministry leaders

- Extended family

- Other parents

- Coaches

- Teacher

**Have family meetings:** These check-ins can provide multiple benefits for your children. Start the family meeting with prayer, then share, talk, and enjoy each other.

- These meetings encourage communication, so you'll have a better idea of how your kids are doing.

- They can help children feel a sense of belonging.

- Family meetings give children a safe place to problem-solve.

- This time together can help you and your children deepen your relationships and create stronger bonds in your home.

# Free online help
## from DivorceCare

### BONUS VIDEOS, ARTICLES, TIPS & DAILY EMAILS JUST FOR YOU

**Access your <u>free</u> DivorceCare resources today!**

**DIVORCECARE.ORG/MY**

# How to watch
## session videos online

Log on to **divorcecare.org/my** to watch full DivorceCare session videos. It's a great option if you:

· Missed a meeting and want to see the video
· Want to rewatch something you saw
· Want to review before your group meeting

**Watch the videos today!**

**DIVORCECARE.ORG/MY**

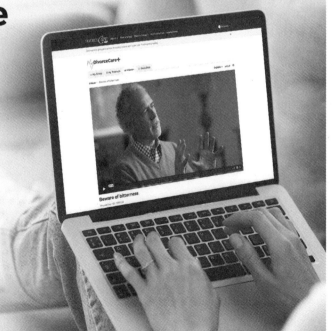

# Anger

*Managing intense displeasure*

It doesn't seem fair. It's not right. So much has happened that just. Makes. Your. Blood. Boil. What are you supposed to do with all this anger?

This week's **video**, **On My Own** exercises, and **My Weekly Journal** will answer that question and provide insights to help you handle this intense emotion. You'll learn:

- **How anger might be helpful in your situation**
- **How anger might be harmful in your situation**
- **How to manage your anger**

# VIDEO OUTLINE

Use this outline to write down important concepts, encouraging words, or questions you may have while viewing the video.

## ANGER CAN BE HURTFUL

## ANGER CAN BE HELPFUL

Anger has a legitimate role

> *"Be angry and do not sin;*
> *do not let the sun*
> *go down on your anger."*
>
> **Ephesians 4:26 ESV**

Anger sets boundaries

Anger is energy for the hard times

## ANGER CAN BE SUBTLE

- In critical comments
- In the silent treatment
- In withholding from people

## ANGER CAN BE MANAGED

Be patient with yourself

Watch out for bitterness

- Do you think I'm bitter?
- Am I wishing my ex harm?
- Am I pulling back from people?
- Am I overreacting?

Avoid venting verbally or physically

*"We know from research that the more you give vent to anger, the more anger you're going to have."*

**Dr. Linda Mintle**

Take time for a deep breath

*"Everyone should be quick to listen, slow to speak and slow to become angry."*

**James 1:19b**

## Use gentle responses

> *"A gentle answer turns away wrath, but a harsh word stirs up anger."*
>
> **Proverbs 15:1**

## Take a time-out

- Pray
- Listen to uplifting music
- Exercise
- Get counsel from a wise friend
- Think through your goals
- Think of it like a business

> *"What causes fights and quarrels among you? Don't they come from your desires that battle within you?"*
>
> **James 4:1**

## Ask yourself some key questions

- Would I teach my children to do this?
- In the bigger scheme of things, what's the best course of action?
- What would someone I look up to do?

> *"Bless them that curse you, do good to them that hate you, and pray for them which despitefully use you."*
>
> **Matthew 5:44b KJV**

## Take your anger to God

### Additional help

**When you want to lash out** —— p. 25

**How do I get control over anger?** — p. 25

**But I'm still angry** —— p. 27

# ON MY *Own*

## *Wisdom and encouragement for your new journey*

### ELSA'S STORY

*"My anger didn't come out in bombs—more like hand grenades. I would snap at my daughter. I'd be driving down the road and someone would cut me off, and I would %#@%#%#. I'd stub my toe, and I'd be cursing. All of this anger was sitting inside me that I didn't want to acknowledge."* Whether your anger tends to explode or lies under the surface at a slow, constant simmer, this week you'll learn how to feel, express, and deal with anger in healthy ways.

## **1** HOW DO I HANDLE ALL THIS ANGER?

Let's face it. Some people know how to push your buttons. And when they do, how well do you handle it? There are many ways to handle anger—and not all of them are good for you. In fact, some responses will hurt you even more than the other person. Even when your anger is justified, God knows it can quickly lead to unhealthy reactions. This is what He wants to help you avoid.

## GOD'S MESSAGE TO YOU

*"Everyone should be quick to listen, slow to speak and slow to become angry."* (James 1:19b)

*"What causes fights and quarrels among you? Don't they come from your desires that battle within you?"* (James 4:1)

1. **What actions or behaviors tend to make you angry? How do you usually respond?**

2. **According to James 1:19, what is the best way to respond?**

3. **James 4:1 talks about desires and motives that create inner conflict, which can spill out and affect your relationships. How do you see this playing out in your life?**

## REMEMBER

- You're going to experience anger. When you do, it's your response that matters.

- Here's what being quick to listen might look like:
    - Not interrupting
    - Not planning your response while the other person is speaking
    - Removing distractions to offer your full attention
    - Confirming your understanding of the other person's point of view, hurts, and desires before sharing your own

*"I have to find a healthy way to deal with [my anger]."* – Chuck

## 2 WHEN YOU WANT TO LASH OUT

Maybe your frustration simmers beneath the surface. You snap at the kids at breakfast. You grumble as your boss gives you yet another responsibility. You find out what your ex did last night and the texts start to fly.

What happens when you react with a quick temper? It might feel like the natural thing to do, but it only ends up making things worse. But God wants good things for you. So, He explains a better way to handle these moments.

## GOD'S MESSAGE TO YOU

*"A gentle answer turns away wrath, but a harsh word stirs up anger."* (Proverbs 15:1)

*"A quick-tempered person does foolish things."* (Proverbs 14:17a)

*"Watch your tongue and keep your mouth shut, and you will stay out of trouble."* (Proverbs 21:23 NLT)

**1. How short is your fuse?**

☐ I tend to be quick-tempered.

☐ I'm patient in some situations, but I get angry and lash out in others.

☐ I can usually hold my tongue and remain calm.

**2. According to Proverbs 15 and 21, what are good ways to respond when you or someone else is angry?**

**3. Think about a scenario in which you regularly get angry. Give an example of a gentle (mild) response you could use when you're tempted to lash out.**

## REMEMBER

- When you feel your temper starting to boil, ask God to help you respond with a gentle answer—or give you the strength to say nothing at all.

- Before you speak, consider: Is what I'm about to say beneficial for everyone involved?

*"Lashing out accomplishes nothing."* – Dr. Stephen Viars

## 3 HOW DO I GET CONTROL OVER MY ANGER?

It's not uncommon to lose your temper when talking to your ex. But it's not the best thing either. What can you do to avoid exploding? Or to avoid shutting down and dodging the issue? If your anger drives you to these types of reactions, which only make the problem worse, it would be appropriate to take a "time-out." Use that time to process your anger and to prepare for addressing the conflict.

## APPLY THE TRUTH

Several years back, Leslie Vernick was looking for a way to control her temper. While reflecting on her problem, she came up with questions to help her manage her anger. See if these questions will help you figure out why you're getting upset and how to respond differently.

| T | What's my **TROUBLE?** | State what's making you angry. |
|---|---|---|
| R | What's my **RESPONSE?** | Is this the best response? You can't control other people's actions, but you can control your response. |
| U | What's going on **UNDERNEATH?** | Check what's motivating you. E.g., is it a desire for control, for respect, or to get your way? |
| T | What's the **TRUTH?** | Your feelings do not always indicate truth. What does the Bible say is true about you, the other person, and your conflict? |
| H | How will my **HEART*** change? | What new perspective do you need to adopt about you, the other person, and your conflict? What preferences do you need to stop insisting upon? |

*Biblically speaking, the heart is the source of a person's values, thoughts, and desires.*

*"I was a fuse waiting to be lit."* – Mary Lou

# WHY SHOULD I GET RID OF MY ANGER?

Take a look at the consequences of anger described in the Bible.

## GOD'S MESSAGE TO YOU

*"For as churning cream produces butter, and as twisting the nose produces blood, so stirring up anger produces strife."* (Proverbs 30:33)

*"An angry person stirs up conflict, and a hot-tempered person commits many sins."* (Proverbs 29:22)

*"**24** Do not make friends with a hot-tempered person, do not associate with one easily angered, **25** or you may learn their ways and get yourself ensnared."* (Proverbs 22:24–25)

1. **Proverbs 30:33 shows that stirring up anger will bring consequences. What is the consequence that's named here? And do you really want more of this in your life?**

2. **What are the effects of your anger, according to Proverbs 29:22?**

3. **Proverbs 22:24–25 describes the effects an angry person will have on others. Based on this passage, how might your children be affected by your unhealthy anger?**

## REMEMBER

- "When you feel the heat rising, you have to be very careful about what you say. You can't take back words, and the damage that does sometimes is irreparable." – Dr. Crawford Loritts

- If you find yourself becoming bitter and angry, ask yourself, "Do I really want to be that kind of person?"

 **5 BUT I'M STILL ANGRY**

Maybe it was one big disagreement. Or maybe 1,000 little ones. Either way, you may find yourself still angry long afterward. You've been hurt, and it's hard to let it go. But holding on to anger isn't doing you any good. In fact, it's hurting you. And you might not realize just how much.

## GOD'S MESSAGE TO YOU

"**26** And 'don't sin [disobey God] by letting anger control you.' Don't let the sun go down while you are still angry, **27** for anger gives a foothold to the devil." (Ephesians 4:26–27 NLT)

1. **Think of a disagreement you're having with someone that hasn't been resolved. How has it been affecting you (e.g., physically, emotionally, behaviorally)?**

2. **Ephesians 4 does not say being angry is necessarily wrong. What does it say about anger?**

3. **Giving "a foothold to the devil" basically means you've created another opportunity for division to occur between you and the other person. According to Ephesians 4, what can you do to prevent another hurtful division in your life?**

## REMEMBER

You can't always fix everything before sunset, but you can commit to resolving disagreements as soon as possible.

You might feel your anger is justified. How can you know for sure? Determine if you're angry about something that offends God. If it is, your anger is warranted—but it's still your responsibility to respond wisely.

## ELSA'S STORY

"Handling anger in a God-honoring way was a process for me. Because I was an avoider, I thought that God wanted me to stuff it down, that I wasn't supposed to be angry. But that's not true. There are things worth being angry about. [I realized] it's okay to be angry about injustices that were done to me and my daughter.

"I'm a journaler, so I would spend a lot of time processing my anger in a journal and talking to God (I am angry about … ). It's like in the Psalms: David would start a psalm ticked off about something, and at the end he is praising God. So acknowledging it, writing about it, and then saying, 'But God, You are good,' is ultimately how I ended up processing anger."

## NEXT SESSION

**How to deal with grief, depression, and guilt.**

# MY WEEKLY Journal

If you find yourself struggling with being irritable, easily frustrated, and quick to "snap" at people in anger, then use your weekly journal to evaluate a recent situation in which you got angry. Here are some statements to get you started:

1. **I got irritated/angry when ...** (Describe the circumstances.)

2. **I did and said ...** (Describe your reactions.)

3. **The outcome was ...** (Describe the consequences of your reaction.)

4. **Based on what the Bible says in passages like James 4:1–3, Proverbs 13:3, and Proverbs 15:18, the outcome might have been better if I had ...**

## CHART YOUR PROGRESS

Place a check in the boxes to identify how you are feeling in each area this week: emotionally, physically, etc. Even better? Substitute a word or two to describe how you are doing.

| | REALLY BAD | OKAY | PRETTY GOOD | GREAT |
|---|---|---|---|---|
| **Emotionally** | | | | |
| **Physically** | | | | |
| **Spiritually** (closeness to God) | | | | |
| **Relationally** (closeness to others) | | | | |
| **How your life is in general** | | | | |

# How to respond to temper tantrums

With separation and divorce come unwanted change, stress, and loss. It's pretty common for your children to be overwhelmed with emotions and for the stress to come out in the form of anger.

Their bucket may be filled to the brim, and one more drop (which might seem like a trivial thing) can make them tip over. The result is angry outbursts at home, at school, and anywhere, really—even at church.

So what are you supposed to do when your child erupts? Here are 10 things you can do to help.

1. **Provide privacy:** If your child is having a meltdown in front of a group, try to separate him from the others. The last thing your child needs in that moment is an audience.

2. **Give comfort:** If possible, give the child comfort at the moment by placing your hand on her shoulder and talking in a low, controlled voice. This might be enough to calm some children.

3. **Describe their response:** If the child is raging, don't try to touch him, but describe what his body is doing: "Your face is going like this. Your shoulders are doing this." When some kids become angry, the fight-or-flight response is in control. They literally can't think beyond how their body is reacting. When you describe what their body is doing, they'll usually turn and re-engage with you.

4. **Offer empathy:** As the child looks at you, show her you can relate to how she is feeling by repeating what she said as a question: "You're upset because you wanted to stay at your dad's today? I understand because sometimes when I get to visit someone, I don't want to come back either."

5. **Ask about helping:** Ask your child, "What can I do to help you?" If the child makes a reasonable request, honor it. If not, simply say, "Hmm, that's not possible. How about if I _____?" and offer another idea.

6. **Offer choices:** As the child settles down, offer two choices, such as rejoining whatever activity was going on or sitting alone for a while.

7. **Try conversation:** Sometimes, right after an emotional explosion is the time children want to talk. This can turn into an intimate time when you can impact the child with love.

8. **Encourage them to rehydrate:** Raging can drain children, and water will help them rehydrate. Offer your child some water, or tell him to get a drink of water. This gives him the chance to move out of the area where he had the rage and allows his brain to move forward with a different thought.

9. **Teach them to breathe:** Deep breathing exercises can help keep your children calm in the future. "Deep breathing" means slowly taking in a breath through the nose while pushing out the belly, and then slowly breathing out through the mouth. Breathing slowly sends calming signals to the brain.

10. **Turn to Scripture:** Offer Scripture for your children to refer to when they are struggling with anger. Here are some ideas:

    • "Be quick to listen, slow to speak and slow to become angry." (James 1:19)

    • "Cast all your anxiety on him because he cares for you." (1 Peter 5:7)

# Grief & DEPRESSION

## *Wisdom for dealing with sadness*

The sadness of loss. Anger over the unfairness of it all. And intense feelings of guilt. Working through the many emotions of grief after your separation or divorce will likely be one of the hardest things you ever have to do. And your divorce recovery can be maddening if your grief morphs into depression.

Digging in to this week's **video**, the daily **On My Own** exercises, and **My Weekly Journal** will help. You'll discover:

- **What to expect in your experience with grief**
- **How to know if your grief has turned into depression**
- **What to do when guilt complicates your grief or depression**
- **How you can grow through your grief or depression**

# VIDEO OUTLINE

Use this outline to write down important concepts, encouraging words, or questions you may have while viewing the video.

## GRIEVING THE LOSSES

## UNDERSTANDING GRIEF

Grief is different for everyone

Grief affects all areas of life

Grief has "triggers" (memories)

Grief has its own timetable

Grief can be like a roller coaster

## MOVING BEYOND GRIEF

Develop a "growth mindset"

*"Your healing journey will include these three things: progress, plateaus, and setbacks."*

**Dr. Ramon Presson**

Look at what you still have

# UNDERSTANDING DEPRESSION

Depression could develop from grief

Depression makes everything a burden

Depression blocks access to happiness

# DEPRESSION CAN INVOLVE

- Loss of interest in fun activities
- More time alone
- Changes in appetite
- Changes in sleep
- Self-critical thoughts
- Hopelessness

# DEPRESSION MAY ALSO INVOLVE

- A negative view of myself
- A negative view of my life
- A negative view of my future

# DEALING WITH DEPRESSION

Counseling can help

Medication might help

## DRAW NEARER TO GOD

Read the Bible, God's Word

Pray to God

Journal

## DEALING WITH GUILT

Ask God for forgiveness

> "But now, this is what the LORD says—he who created you, Jacob, he who formed you, Israel: 'Do not fear, for I have redeemed you; I have summoned you by name; you are mine. When you pass through the waters, I will be with you; and when you pass through the rivers, they will not sweep over you. When you walk through the fire, you will not be burned; the flames will not set you ablaze.'"
>
> **Isaiah 43:1–2**

> "Pray about everything. Tell God what you need, and thank him for all he has done."
>
> **Philippians 4:6b NLT**

### Additional help

12 tips for better rest ———— p. 35

I feel hopeless. What now? ——— p. 36

A grace that's bigger than guilt —— p. 37

# ON MY *Own*

## Wisdom and encouragement for your new journey

### DETRICK'S STORY

*"In the beginning of my divorce I felt a lot of guilt and shame because of my actions. It took a toll on me. I got depressed. I stayed away from church. For about two months I didn't go at all because I was kind of beating myself up at what happened."* A combination of guilt and grief might be taking its toll on your day-to-day living. This week's exercises will help you learn how to work through your emotions and point you toward new hope for your future.

## 1  12 TIPS FOR BETTER REST

If you're struggling with grief or depression, restless nights and lack of sleep might be the norm for you. Here's how much sleep the National Sleep Foundation[2] recommends per night:

| Age range | Recommended daily range |
|---|---|
| 18–25 years | 7–9 hours |
| 26–64 years | 7–9 hours |
| 65+ years | 7–8 hours |

These suggestions may help you sleep better:[3]

1. **Be consistent:** Keep a consistent sleep schedule. Get up at the same time every day, even on weekends or during vacations.

2. **Time it right:** Don't go to bed unless you're sleepy.

3. **Don't fight it:** If you don't fall asleep after 20 minutes, get out of bed.

4. **Make it routine:** Establish a relaxing bedtime routine (e.g., play soothing or comforting music).

5. **Create a device-free zone:** Use your bed only for sleep (rather than looking at your phone or computer, watching TV, etc.).

6. **Set the stage:** Make your bedroom ideal for sleep. Keep it quiet and relaxing, and keep the room at a comfortable, cool temperature.

7. **Limit exposure to light:** Try to avoid exposure to bright light in the evenings.

8. **Unplug:** Turn off electronic devices at least 30 minutes before bedtime.

9. **Eat early:** Don't eat a large meal before bedtime. If you're hungry at night, eat a light, healthy snack.

10. **Stay fit:** Exercise regularly and maintain a healthy diet.

11. **Cut off caffeine:** Avoid consuming caffeine in the late afternoon or evening.

12. **Reduce restroom runs:** Drink fewer fluids before bedtime.

## 2. I FEEL HOPELESS. WHAT NOW?

Sure, your future has never been certain, but at least you had some plans in place. Since the separation or divorce, you may feel like your plans have been ripped to shreds. Maybe you need a new place to live. Relationships are changing, and you might feel abandoned by friends or family. And living on your own might seem impossible on your solo income.

Trying to face all these difficulties at once is no doubt overwhelming. It may even seem pointless or hopeless to go on. From where you're standing, that way of thinking might make sense, and suicide might seem like the only option. But it's not.

### HOPE IS POSSIBLE

The comforting fact is, others have gone through the struggles you're facing—and survived! Although that fact doesn't change your current situation, it's an important reminder that hope is possible, even now.

What you need is a different point of view to see your way out of the darkness and chaos in your life. There is

always someone to talk to about your struggle. Here are some contacts you can reach out to for some immediate help:

- Your local police
- Your physician
- Your local fire station
- The nearest emergency room
- A pastor of a local church

If you can't talk to a person right away in your area, then call the National Suicide Prevention Lifeline:

**800-273-8255**

You don't have to face those dark times alone.

## 3. A NEW KIND OF HOPE

When the weight of grief and sadness feels like it's crushing your spirit, you need hope. Not the wishful thinking or roll-of-the-dice hope that our culture often promotes, but a confident hope, grounded and secure. This is the hope that God offers.

### GOD'S MESSAGE TO YOU

*"18 So God has given both his promise and his oath. These two things are unchangeable because it is impossible for God to lie. Therefore, we who have fled to him for refuge can have great confidence as we hold to the hope that lies before us. 19 This hope is a strong and trustworthy anchor for our souls."* (Hebrews 6:18–19a NLT)

1. **How would you define the word "hope"?**

2. **How does Hebrews 6 describe hope?**

3. "Hope" looks into the future. The hope talked about in the Bible is certain, assured. So even in the midst of suffering and challenges, what God promises you will most certainly happen. If you had this kind of hope, how would that change your response to your situation?

## REMEMBER

- Biblical hope is a confident expectation rooted in the character of God.

- Other sources of hope can let you down, but God does not lie or fail. When things feel hopeless, you can trust in God's promises.

- Fixing your eyes on God's promises is always better than focusing on your problems.

## 4 NO LONGER GUILTY

*This isn't what I had planned for my life.*
*I have so many regrets.*
*I feel guilty—and ashamed.*

Loss and sadness after a divorce are often accompanied by regret. Regret can lead to guilt and shame. And if you don't deal with guilt and shame, they can block your recovery process. They can keep you from the peace God has for you. But here's the good news: Whatever is in your past, God can wipe your record clean. He can remove all guilt and shame by declaring you "not guilty" and giving you the freedom to live in joy.

## GOD'S MESSAGE TO YOU

*"If we confess our sins, he is faithful and just and will forgive us our sins and purify us from all unrighteousness."* (1 John 1:9)

*"Blessed is the one whose sin the LORD does not count against them."* (Psalm 32:2a)

1. What past events are causing you to feel guilt or shame?

2. If we truly are guilty of a wrongdoing, and we seek God's forgiveness through Jesus, He is the one who can free us from that sin and the guilt and shame that often accompany it. According to today's verses, what can you do to be purified (cleansed) of sin and guilt? And what are the benefits of doing that?

## REMEMBER

- The weight of guilt and shame is heavy, but you don't have to carry it anymore. God has made a way, through His forgiveness, to remove your guilt and shame.

- God is ready to forgive you and give you a fresh start—today. See page 103 to learn how this is possible.

*"These consequences are not permanent definers of what I can be."* – Dr. Crawford Loritts

## 5 A GRACE THAT'S BIGGER THAN YOUR GUILT

"I blamed myself. [After divorce] you can think of a dozen things you should have done differently or you should have done better," says Mike.

The guilt can be overwhelming. If you're not careful, it can take you to a place of despair. But it is possible to go the opposite direction—toward hope. First, find out what the Bible says about your guilt. (Have you actually done something wrong and violated the Bible's teaching? Or do you feel guilty because you violated your own standard or any other lesser standard?)

Second, overcome your guilt by embracing God's truth. The truth is, if you're a Christian, there's nothing you can do to make God love you more, or less: No matter what has happened, God sees you as His beloved child.

How can that be? When you brought your sins (wrongs) to Him, He washed your past, present, and future record clean. Plus, God credited Christ's perfect, sinless life to your account. So He counts you as His perfect, sinless child. So the next time you feel like God won't love you because you don't meet His standards, remind yourself that God accepts you because of what Christ did on your behalf.

## PUTTING IT INTO PRACTICE

What direction are your thoughts taking you? To keep moving toward hope, try this:

- Post a picture of an eraser where you'll see it regularly.

- Memorize 2 Corinthians 5:17 or write it next to the eraser picture: "Anyone who belongs to Christ has become a new person. The old life is gone; a new life has begun!" (NLT)

Go back to these any time you need a reminder that God wipes away your guilt with His grace.

*"God does forgive and restore."* – Detrick

# DETRICK'S STORY

*"I know my actions led to a lot of issues in my marriage, and I can't go back and change those actions. Moving forward, I can't beat myself up about it—which is hard when [my ex-wife] continuously brings up the past.*

*"Yes, I did some things wrong, but God forgives and restores. For me, what it means for God to have forgiven me is that He washes away my sins. It doesn't mean I won't have negative consequences for what I did, but He does forgive me, and I am able to move forward and make better choices."*

## NEXT SESSION

How to handle loneliness after separation or divorce.

# MY WEEKLY
## Journal

In your grief (and possibly depression), use your weekly journal to write your experiences. Here are some statements to help you get started.

1. **My grief (or depression) was intense recently when …**

2. **During that time, my thoughts were focused on the following concerns, losses, disappointments, etc. …**

3. **What I learned from the video and On My Own exercises that helps me with those thoughts is …**

## CHART YOUR PROGRESS

Place a check in the boxes to identify how you are feeling in each area this week: emotionally, physically, etc. Even better? Substitute a word or two to describe how you are doing.

| | REALLY BAD | OKAY | PRETTY GOOD | GREAT |
|---|---|---|---|---|
| **Emotionally** | | | | |
| **Physically** | | | | |
| **Spiritually** (closeness to God) | | | | |
| **Relationally** (closeness to others) | | | | |
| **How your life is in general** | | | | |

# Your kids are grieving too
## How to help them manage their grief

When it's hard to understand everything going on in your own heart, it might feel impossible to understand your children's grief experience. How do you help them work through their grief—while dealing with your own? Try these steps:

### 1. Be real with your kids

You don't want to burden your children. So you hide your sadness and grieve in isolation. But Ron L. Deal explains: "This isn't helpful to them. You want to show strength, but showing strength is being real about your sadness. It's being real with your questions and struggles. Your kids are probably having some of the same struggles."

Dr. Linda Mintle recommends setting an example for how to handle sadness in a healthy way. You can be sad and cry with your children to show them it's okay to express their emotions, but don't overwhelm them. If you need to wail, do so when you're alone with God.

Your honesty lets your kids know it's safe to be sad with you. They can process their feelings with someone who loves them.

- Being open and honest about your grief lets your children know it's okay for them to grieve too.

### 2. Help your kids understand the changes

Your children are probably trying to figure out what life looks like now—because it sure doesn't look like it used to. They have confusing thoughts they don't know how to express. They'll probably have misunderstandings about what has happened. To help them, engage them in conversations.

Start by asking about what's going on in their life. Talk about specific events or activities rather than about general, abstract concepts. Inquire about their behaviors, thoughts, or words. Don't ask children how they feel about something that happened. Many children don't know how they feel, and they need an adult to help them discover and label their feelings.

Be patient with children's misunderstandings; showing frustration or shock will more likely shut down further conversation. Don't assume a misunderstanding will be corrected by one conversation. Correct their misunderstandings with concise explanations. And it's best to avoid figurative language and clichés.

- Children will need your help understanding the changes in their lives.

### 3. Understand they'll revisit the loss as they age

Your children will revisit the losses associated with divorce at later points in their lives, though they won't necessarily grieve with the same intensity or duration.

"Kids grieve developmentally," Deal says. They may process their losses at different times as they mature. For example, a nine-year-old boy may grieve that Mom and Dad can't both come to his ball game. As a teenager, he might fear the thought of dating and marriage because his parents' relationship ended in divorce.

- Grief can show up in different ways at various stages of your children's lives.

### Putting it into practice

Use one-on-one time with children to have meaningful conversations about how they're doing. These phrases can start or guide the conversation:

- It's okay to feel sad right now. I do, too.

- What do you think will help you feel better?

- I realize this is a tough time for you.

- Change can be hard. How are you doing with all the changes?

- Going to God is the best thing we can do when we're sad. Let's pray together and ask for help.

# Loneliness

## Overcoming feelings of isolation

Where your marriage relationship once was, there's now a gaping hole—and it's easy for loneliness to creep into that space. You may wonder if you should fill that hole with other people, embrace the solitude, or make the TV your new best friend.

This week, through the **video**, the daily **On My Own** exercises, and **My Weekly Journal**, you'll discover:

- **Why loneliness hurts so much**
- **What temptations to avoid in your loneliness**
- **The best ways to overcome loneliness**

## VIDEO OUTLINE

Use this outline to write down important concepts, encouraging words, or questions you may have while viewing the video.

### WHY LONELINESS HURTS

> *"God has wired us to connect. He's hardwired human beings to connect with other human beings."*
>
> **Leslie Vernick**

### AVOID ISOLATING YOURSELF

Avoid unwise use of media

- Beware of late-night texting
- Select your music wisely
- Turn off the TV

### AVOID ROMANTIC CONNECTIONS

### FOLLOW GOD'S DESIGN FOR SEX

> *"Sex is God's creation. It's His idea; it's His gift to us."*
>
> **Tray Lovvorn**

## A SOLUTION FOR LONELINESS

Develop relationships of mutual care

Spend meaningful time with your children

Serve others in need

Challenge yourself with personal growth

## RECONNECT WITH GOD

- Listen to worship music
- Read Scripture
- Pray
- Spend time with others

## JOURNAL WHAT YOU'RE LEARNING

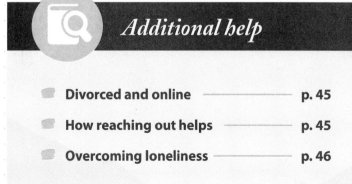

### Additional help

# ON MY *Own*

*Wisdom and encouragement for your new journey*

## CONNIE'S STORY

*"At night was probably the loneliest time because my daughter was in bed. I would be faced with thoughts of, It's just me and her. And every day I had to face a new day with those same thoughts again. I realized, if I'm not careful, loneliness is something I could drown myself in."* This week you'll discover, as Connie did, how to transform lonely days into fulfilling moments.

## 1 ISOLATION OR SOLITUDE?

Social media bombards you with images. It looks like everyone is out there doing fun things—while you're home, alone.

Did you know solitude can be a good thing? That it can be healthy to pursue alone time? Vaneetha found intentional solitude to be helpful: Six months after her husband left, she went to a Christian retreat center. For 24 hours, she didn't say a word to anyone, but spent the time in reflection and prayer. Vaneetha says, "Life is full of noise. I felt a sense of peace and release and just being with God."

It can be life-giving to be alone. You could be alone and be sad, or you could use the time well, such as for reading, painting, praying, or another personally meaningful activity. Maybe you can't get away for an entire weekend, but you can still carve out an hour here and there to take advantage of some solitude.

## SEEK OUT SOLITUDE

List three things you could do with alone time to create your own "silent retreat."

## TAKE A "WOW" WALK

Che-Von shares a different way to use time alone for her benefit: "I've learned how to see my alone time as a gift. I go for 'wow' walks. As I'm walking, I'm looking for interesting things. [E.g., *Wow! That flower is amazing. That house is beautiful.*] I'm not talking on the phone. I'm just walking and noticing at least three things that are beautiful."

Take a "wow" walk today. Write down three things you find:

*"I had to learn to enjoy my own company."* – Mary Lou

# DIVORCED AND ONLINE

"You spend all weekend chatting [online] with people you don't really know. Meanwhile, you're not meeting people you could have real relationships with and getting involved where you can grow and serve," says Leslie Vernick.

Social media can both help and hurt relationships. After separation or divorce, it can help you stay in touch with people who can rally around you as you need support. But you could also end up getting hurt through social media.

## INSTANT DATING

Dr. Stephen Viars explains, "One of the challenges is that a person who's gone through a divorce can almost instantly get into another relationship via the internet. That can be risky because people can present themselves online in a way that is different from who they really are."

## FEEDING MY INSECURITIES

Omar King adds, "More and more people are afraid to have face-to-face conversations because they're so accustomed to interacting with people via social media. It's a skill that if you don't practice it, you lose it, and that can make you feel insecure."

Yet, social media can also help you stay in touch with loved ones when you need them most. So, should you use it or avoid it?

## WHAT'S MY MOTIVATION?

Think about *why* you use social media. Is it an attempt to avoid feeling alone or avoid the challenges of face-to-face conversations? Are you longing to find

someone to date who might make you feel good about yourself temporarily—before you've done the work of healing?

Self-assess your social media use:

1. What do you hope to accomplish when you post on social media?

2. What are two things you could do to limit the time you spend on social media and connect with people face-to-face instead?

# HOW REACHING OUT HELPS

Have you ever been in a room full of people, yet felt lonelier than ever? Simply being around people is not a surefire cure for loneliness.

What can make these times more meaningful and allow you to create connections is reaching out to others in small, caring ways. As you share a simple meal, offer to drive an elderly person to get groceries, or send an encouraging note to a friend, you are healing some of the loneliness in someone else's life, which can also heal yours. This simple act of being friendly and sharing what you have is what the Bible calls "hospitality."

## GOD'S MESSAGE TO YOU

"**10** Be devoted to one another in love. Honor one another above yourselves. … **13** Share with the Lord's people who are in need. Practice hospitality." (Romans 12:10, 13)

"Offer hospitality to one another without grumbling." (1 Peter 4:9)

1. **Write about a time when someone welcomed you into his or her home or met a basic need. What was your reaction? Do you know how it affected your host?**

2. **According to this week's verses, what attitudes are necessary to connect with other people in a healthy way?**

3. **Name someone who might be feeling down or stressed. Plan an act of kindness you could do for that person.**

## REMEMBER

- Being created in God's image means you were designed to help and serve others. When you aren't serving others on a regular basis, you'll feel like something is missing from your life.

- If you're feeling lonely, offering hospitality is a way God has provided to make meaningful connections in your life.

*"I know I can't stay here and deal with this loneliness by myself."* – Detrick

## **4 OVERCOMING LONELINESS**

Your friends may invite you to spend time with them: "Come ON. It'll be fun!" Part of you wants to go—you *have* been feeling lonely—but sweatpants and TV sound easier. Plus, some friends will turn the night into a spouse-bashing fest. And others will want to keep things so lighthearted that you can't be honest about your hurts.

But there is another possibility. In the Bible, God calls it Christian "fellowship." It's where friends get together to encourage one another—supporting and uplifting each other through life's ups and downs.

## GOD'S MESSAGE TO YOU

*"**24** And let us consider how we may spur one another on toward love and good deeds, **25** not giving up meeting together, as some are in the habit of doing, but encouraging one another."* (Hebrews 10:24–25a)

1. **Today's verses describe fellowship—God's design for friendship between people who believe in Jesus.* What does He want friends to do when they get together?**

*"Christian believers" are people who trust in what Jesus did to save them from their sins (wrongs) and to give them the gift of eternal life. Learn more on page ix.*

2. **When you get together with your friends, which of those things typically happen?**

3. **Friendship goes two ways. Rate how you've been doing (1 being "I'm completely focused on myself"; 10 being "I'm regularly in the habit of doing what's described in Hebrews 10").**

| 1 | 2 | 3 | 4 | 5 | 6 | 7 | 8 | 9 | 10 |

## REMEMBER

- Fellowship relieves loneliness.

- You can use friendships with Christians to encourage and be encouraged.

- Meeting together on a regular basis gives Christian believers the chance to remind one another of God's love and forgiveness.

*"Am I going to be this way forever?"* – Sally

## 5   I LONG FOR INTIMACY

If you long for an intimate connection with someone, it might seem reasonable to fill that ache with sexual relationships. But, as you pursue these connections, you can hurt your relationship with God. Because God loves you, He doesn't want anything to come between you and Him. So He gives guidance about sexual purity.

## GOD'S MESSAGE TO YOU

*"3 It is God's will that you should be sanctified [purified/ freed from sin]: that you should avoid sexual immorality; 4 that each of you should learn to control your own body in a way that is holy and honorable. … 7 For God did not call us to be impure, but to live a holy life. 8 Therefore, anyone who rejects this instruction does not reject a human being but God."* (1 Thessalonians 4:3–4, 7–8a)

1. **Sex outside of marriage creates a distance between God and you. It will never fulfill your loneliness—because God didn't design it to. What are other possible complications of having sex with someone you're not married to?**

2. **According to this passage, what is God's will for you?**

3. **What happens if you reject God's instructions about staying pure?** (See verse 8.)

## REMEMBER

- It's tempting to think of sex simply as a physical act between two consenting adults. But if you are a Christian, sinful sexual activity negatively affects your relationship with God.

- To live the better life God wants for you, He calls you to remain pure because He is pure, and He will give you the power to do so.

### BRIGHTER DAYS

## CONNIE'S STORY

*"I started teaching art to homeschoolers. It filled up the nights so I wouldn't be lonely. I also started working as a church financial secretary. That put me around supportive people.*

*"Through all this, I've learned the greatest solution to loneliness is serving other people. And when you're struggling, be careful about being around people that are negative. The best thing to do is to surround yourself with positive people who are forward-thinking about your life."*

## NEXT SESSION

Explore ways to move beyond fear and worry.

# MY WEEKLY *Journal*

Maybe you don't like to be by yourself, which is understandable. But when you are, it's good to use that time to reflect on what you're learning about yourself and God. The following prompts can help guide your reflections.

1. **One thing I've learned about myself when I've been alone is …**

2. **One thing I would profit from doing when I'm alone is … because …**

3. **What I learned from the video and On My Own exercises about God that could help me when I'm alone is …**

## CHART YOUR PROGRESS

Place a check in the boxes to identify how you are feeling in each area this week: emotionally, physically, etc. Even better? Substitute a word or two to describe how you are doing.

|  | REALLY BAD | OKAY | PRETTY GOOD | GREAT |
|---|---|---|---|---|
| **Emotionally** |  |  |  |  |
| **Physically** |  |  |  |  |
| **Spiritually** (closeness to God) |  |  |  |  |
| **Relationally** (closeness to others) |  |  |  |  |
| **How your life is in general** |  |  |  |  |

# FOR Parents

## *My children miss my former spouse*
### Helping them deal with loneliness

*"The day my dad moved out was the loneliest day in my life!"*

*"I can't go to my mom's house for spring break because she's taking a vacation with her boyfriend and his kids."*

*"I used to be really lonely when I got home from school at 3, because my dad didn't get home until 5."*

Co-parenting is hard. Single parenting can be even harder. Among the many challenges is the loneliness your children may experience as they miss the other parent. What can you do to help your children with this ache? Here are five ideas:

### 1. Explain

Especially for younger children, it's good to explain what loneliness is. Give them words to use so they can express what they're feeling.

### 2. Encourage

Kids struggling with loneliness could use some encouragement. Send them texts to check in. Tell them you love them. Give them a chance to talk about their day-to-day experiences—and really listen.

### 3. Equip

Provide examples from the Bible about people who lost, were abandoned by, or were betrayed by their family and friends (David, Job, Jesus). Give children Scriptures they can read and memorize to help them with loneliness, such as:

- "I am with you always." (Matthew 28:20b)

- "Nothing … will ever be able to separate us from the love of God that is revealed in Christ Jesus our Lord." (Romans 8:39b NLT)

- "[God] will neither fail you nor abandon you." (Deuteronomy 31:6b NLT)

### 4. Entertain

There may be times when your children are home alone before or after school or on weekends. When children feel lonely, they can turn to unhealthy habits to keep themselves entertained. Excessive use of video games can become an addiction that kids get caught in as they try to escape their loneliness.

Try to limit the amount of screen time your kids have each day. Encourage them to play board games or read, or suggest creative outlets like painting, dancing, or building. Try to nudge them toward more physical and interactive activities and away from extensive gaming.

### 5. Embrace

This doesn't have to be a physical embrace (although a big hug now and then can be a great comfort to children). The idea here is to embrace them relationally. If you're co-parenting, or working two jobs as a single parent to support your kids, it can be hard to spend enough time with children to develop a deep relationship—but it's not impossible. Don't settle for a surface relationship.

This might mean going out less socially with friends or on dates. It might mean doing things you don't enjoy that much, like playing kiddie games, going to a sporting event, or reading your child's favorite book for the 100th time. The point is to be intentional about setting aside quality time with your kids. Find ways to connect, so they know they're not alone.

# SPEED ZONE *Ahead*

## — *Be careful of accelerating into a new relationship* —

**I**ntimacy is a huge part of marriage. What am I supposed to do to fill that void?" says Kimberly. It's tough when the pain is raw, and it seems like a little human connection could ease your hurt and fill that physical and emotional void.

That's why people often jump into a sexual or dating relationship after separation or divorce. Ron L. Deal explains: "We turn toward whatever makes us feel good or numbs the pain. People turn toward rebound relationships, and it just makes things worse."

## SLOW DOWN AND FOCUS ON HEALING

What's worse than the pain from that void? Being in a new relationship that ends up hurting you even more because you rushed—because it felt good at the time.

"You're feeling lonely, and you think the cure is to find another person to be with," says Dr. Stephen Viars. "But you still have a lot of emotions you need to deal with first. Unresolved issues will be detrimental to that new relationship." You are going through a healing process, and your focus needs to be on your health and growth—finding the tools and developing the confidence to get you through future trials.

## HERE'S WHERE TO START

King David experienced betrayal and loss due to broken relationships. If you're looking to fill a desire for physical and emotional intimacy, follow David's example and start by praying these words to God: "Turn to me and be gracious to me, for I am lonely and afflicted. Relieve the troubles of my heart and free me from my anguish" (Psalm 25:16–17). David continued to cry out to God with his hurts and longings. And he continued to declare that his hope is in God.

## REPLACING THE VOID

After her divorce, Kimberly thought about what to do with her desire for physical and emotional closeness and how to stop feeling so empty.

Kimberly decided to deepen her relationship with God, to be intentional about serving and helping others, and to make the effort to grow into a healthier individual. "Even though I lost intimacy in marriage, I gained it in my faith. I've increased my service. And when I hear a sermon, I think how it affects me as a mother and a professional; it helps build me into the woman I need to be."

Through prayer and a relationship with God—through intentional choices for growth and health and serving others—you, too, will find an effective way to address your desire for intimacy.

# Fears & ANXIETY

## Facing the future with confidence and hope

*What's going on? What's going to happen next? What am I gonna do now?* The questions, doubts, what-ifs, and worries can be all-consuming. Fear and anxiety can paralyze you and prevent you from moving forward.

This week's **video**, daily **On My Own** exercises, and **My Weekly Journal** will help you discover:

- How to stop worrying so much
- The best way to deal with an immediate threat
- When it's wise to consider medication

# VIDEO OUTLINE

Use this outline to write down important concepts, encouraging words, or questions you may have while viewing the video.

## COMMON FEARS

## RESPONDING TO THREATS

## INVOLVING THE POLICE

Provide them with the details

Give them written or digital records or pictures

## TAKE YOUR WORRY TO GOD

The problem with worry

Relying on God

Trusting God as your provider

> "Be anxious for nothing, but in everything by prayer and supplication, with thanksgiving, let your requests be made known to God."
>
> **Philippians 4:6 NKJV**

Living in the present

Nurturing gratitude daily

## SLEEP & EXERCISE

## USING MEDICATIONS WISELY

Use them to help with physical symptoms

Don't use them to avoid problems

### Additional help

I can't stop worrying ———————— p. 54

Walk away from anxiety—literally — p. 55

When thoughts spiral out of control — p. 56

# ON MY *Own*

## Wisdom and encouragement for your new journey

### VICKILYNN'S STORY

*"I was up at night with palpitations and sweats. The more I thought about my fear of the future and the unknown, the more I dissected all the bad things that could happen—the more I became anxious. It was eating me alive, and I didn't know how to deal with it."* With so much on your mind, it's easy for anxiety to consume you. This week's exercises will help you reevaluate your fears and teach you practical ways to cope with anxiety.

## 1 I CAN'T STOP WORRYING

When you face hard decisions and new responsibilities after separation or divorce, it's easy to become weary with worry. *My car's barely running. My job is stressing me out. I don't know if I can scrape together money for the bills. I've never had to do _____ before!*

You may be wondering how you're going to handle it all. But there's another way to face each day.

## GOD'S MESSAGE TO YOU

"**25** *That is why I tell you not to worry about everyday life—whether you have enough food and drink, or enough clothes to wear. … 26 Look at the birds. They don't plant or harvest or store food in barns, for your heavenly Father feeds them. And aren't you far more valuable to him than they are? …*

"**34** *So don't worry about tomorrow, for tomorrow will bring its own worries. Today's trouble is enough for today."* (Matthew 6:25–26, 34 NLT)

**1. In the chart below:**

   **a.** List your top three worries this week.

   **b.** Is this concern your direct responsibility? Answer Y/N.

   **c.** How much control do you have over it? Rate 1–10 (1 = no control, 10 = full control).

| TOP 3 WORRIES THIS WEEK | Responsible for this? | Level of control? |
| --- | --- | --- |
| | | |
| | | |
| | | |

Download the chart at **divorcecare.org/my** to reuse.

2. What resources do you have to address those concerns? Where could you get the resources you don't have yet?

3. According to today's verses, why does Jesus say you shouldn't worry about tomorrow?

## REMEMBER

It's hard to deal with each day when you have anxiety over what the next one will bring. So when worry hits, focus on how God is providing today.

God values you. He is committed to providing everything you need to accomplish what He wants you to do.

*"The biggest fear was just being able to provide for my kids."* – Jonathon

## 2  WALK AWAY FROM ANXIETY—LITERALLY

Anxiety puts stress on your body. And exercise is a good way to relieve that stress and reduce its negative effects. The good news is, you don't necessarily have to jog, lift weights, or play sports. Other physical activities, such as working in your yard, housecleaning, and playing with the kids, can help lower your stress and anxiety.

Walking outdoors is another great option. Here are some tips from the American Heart Association to get the best results from walking:[4]

- **Consult your doctor:** If you haven't exercised in a while, see your physician first.

- **Start small:** Begin with short distances, then gradually increase them.

- **Get comfy:** Wear comfortable clothes and supportive shoes (leave half an inch of room for your toes). Dress in layers, so you can adjust as your body temperature rises.

- **Warm up:** Walk at an easy pace for the first several minutes. Then gradually increase your speed.

- **Use good posture:** Keep your head lifted and shoulders relaxed. Swing your arms naturally.

- **Pace yourself:** If you can't talk or catch your breath while walking, slow down.

- **Keep things interesting:** As you become more comfortable with your walking routine, add variety and challenge. You might alternate walking faster and then slower or get adventurous and include hills or stairs.

- **S-t-r-e-t-c-h:** After walking, stretch your legs, shoulders, and back. Hold each stretch for 15 to 30 seconds.

## KEEP AT IT

Walk whenever you can. Try to accumulate a total of 30 minutes by the end of the day. That might mean a few short walks a day. When you can fit them in, longer walks are good for improving your stamina. And the more you're able to reduce stress, the healthier you'll be over time.

## 3  NO LONGER CONTROLLED BY FEAR

Have you considered how your fears might be controlling your actions and responses? Fears about what your ex is going to do next. How he or she is going to respond to your words. Anxieties about your job, your kids.

"I didn't realize how much fear was controlling me," says Joy. But after her divorce, she discovered a way to stop fear from controlling her life. She surrounded herself with God's promises. She posted Bible verses all over her house.

These verses reminded her of who God is, which helped her live by faith, rather than fear.

### 1. God's reliability

- *"God is not human, that he should lie, not a human being, that he should change his mind."* (Numbers 23:19a)

- *"He is the Rock, his works are perfect, and all his ways are just. A faithful God who does no wrong."* (Deuteronomy 32:4a)

### 2. God's faithfulness

- *"The LORD, the LORD, the compassionate and gracious God, slow to anger, abounding in love and faithfulness."* (Exodus 34:6b)

- *"For the word of the LORD is right and true; he is faithful in all he does."* (Psalm 33:4)

### 3. God's love

- *"This is love: not that we loved God, but that he loved us and sent his Son as an atoning sacrifice for our sins."* (1 John 4:10)

- *"For great is his love toward us, and the faithfulness of the LORD endures forever."* (Psalm 117:2a)

## PUTTING FEARS IN THEIR PLACE

Write several of today's verses on sticky notes or on your phone—someplace you'll see them daily—as a reminder that focusing on God puts fears in perspective.

*"Sometimes we can get anxious about our anxiety."*
– Dr. Craig Keener

## 4 WHEN THOUGHTS SPIN OUT OF CONTROL ...

Can you imagine having a heart and mind filled with peace, despite the chaos going on around you? Even when the kids are screaming or the ex is calling, and your body is just … so … tired. Because of God, you can experience security and stability, even when your circumstances are lousy.

## GOD'S MESSAGE TO YOU

*"6 Do not be anxious about anything, but in every situation, by prayer and petition [asking about personal needs], with thanksgiving, present your requests to God. 7 And the peace of God, which transcends all understanding, will guard your hearts and your minds in Christ Jesus."* (Philippians 4:6–7, emphasis added)

1. **When you feel anxious about something, what do you typically do to try and relieve it?**

2. **From these Bible verses, what is something God says you can do when you feel anxious?**

3. **According to verse 6, what is a crucial attitude to develop as you think about your life and bring your anxieties to God? Why might this be so valuable?**

4. **According to verse 7, what kind of reassurance can you find in God?**

## REMEMBER

- Your circumstances don't need to dictate whether or not you have peace. Even amid the chaos, peace is found in God—in who God is and what He has done for you.

- If you're not sure what God has done for you personally, see page ix to read about something you can be very thankful for.

*"I would be up at 3 or 4 a.m. thinking—what am I going to do?"* – Vickilynn

## 5 AFRAID OF GETTING HURT AGAIN

People can hurt us—severely. And after you've been hurt, you may fear what people could do to you next.

As those around you repeatedly do wrong and hurtful things, your anxiety can build until it controls you. King David is a man in the Bible who had many people twist his words, slander him, and be unfaithful to him. How did David handle his hurts and fears?

## GOD'S MESSAGE TO YOU

*"**3** But when I am afraid, I will put my trust in you. **4** I praise God for what he has promised. I trust in God, so why should I be afraid? What can mere mortals do to me?"* (Psalm 56:3–4 NLT)

How could David be so confident when his circumstances were so negative? At these times David counted on God's promise to bless him and his family. David also knew that no person could keep God from accomplishing His purposes—after all, no one is more powerful than God! So, even when his situation was bleak, David had good reasons to remind himself, "God has this covered."

1. **What people do you put up your guard around—fearing that they might hurt you in some way?**

2. **Does your perspective on your situation assume that other people are more powerful than God? How can you follow David's example in your life?**

## REMEMBER

- God is committed to taking care of you and your family. We might not know the details of God's plan, but like David, we can renew our trust in Him.

- Reminding yourself that no person can interfere with God's plan for you can give you peace in the midst of conflict.

*"Part of managing anxiety is accepting that you're experiencing it."* – Dr. Brad Hambrick

### BRIGHTER DAYS

## VICKILYNN'S STORY

*"As a believer, I thought, I shouldn't fear. That means I must not love God. But after talking to other people who have been through divorce and separation, I realized it's pretty common to feel that way and [that I need] to give myself some grace to let myself heal, and trust that God is going to help me through it.*

*"Now I just run to God and say, 'I don't know what else to do but trust You.' I sometimes still feel fear and anxiety, but I'm learning to take it to the Lord and ask Him to help me with it."*

### NEXT SESSION

Sort through the changes in your relationships.

# MY WEEKLY Journal

Fear and anxiety can build and overtake your day. If you're burdened with these emotions, unload them into your journal. And then, by reflecting on and trusting in some of God's promises, you'll be better able to overcome your anxiety in the future.

**1. This week I am feeling anxious about …**

**2. Typically when I start to feel anxious, I …**

**3. I've learned from the video and On My Own exercises that a good way to handle fear and anxiety is to …**

As part of your journaling, review and meditate on the following verses to help calm your fears:

- 1 Peter 5:7
- Deuteronomy 31:6
- Psalm 118:6–9

## CHART YOUR PROGRESS

Place a check in the boxes to identify how you are feeling in each area this week: emotionally, physically, etc. Even better? Substitute a word or two to describe how you are doing.

|  | REALLY BAD | OKAY | PRETTY GOOD | GREAT |
|---|---|---|---|---|
| Emotionally |  |  |  |  |
| Physically |  |  |  |  |
| Spiritually (closeness to God) |  |  |  |  |
| Relationally (closeness to others) |  |  |  |  |
| How your life is in general |  |  |  |  |

## *Help your kids overcome their fears*

I'm scared!" Maybe you've heard these words if your child is afraid of the dark. But when it comes to divorce or separation, those fears might not be so clear. A child's response to worries and anxieties might not look like fear at all. And since children might not understand their own emotions, explaining them to Mom or Dad may seem impossible.

So how can you help your kids with their fears?

### Understand that they may feel unsafe

When children are afraid, their natural response is to expect adults to protect them and keep them safe. But children with divorced parents may have lost a sense of trust in the very people who are supposed to keep them safe. Because of this, they can experience intense safety issues.

And when their world has been shaken and they no longer feel safe, day-to-day activities can be very hard. The fight-or-flight instinct often takes over (which is a natural human response to a perceived threat—to either resist or run). What can look like defiant, rebellious behavior—as they struggle to face school, homework, church, friends, and family—is really just the child feeling scared.

Recognizing this is an important part of helping your children deal with their fears. Keep in mind that children can't connect with others, learn, and interact in healthy ways when they don't feel safe. If they are acting out, regressing, or withdrawing, you may need to respond less with discipline and more with reassurance that they are safe and loved.

### Help them process their fears

Take steps to help them work through what they're feeling. You can start with these three.

1. **Don't ignore their fear.** Encourage your children to talk. At a calm moment, sit down with them and ask them what they know about what's going on with Mom and Dad and what they want to know. Give them the freedom to ask questions and express any concerns, and then respond to them in a calm, reassuring way.

2. **Observe their play.** Children may use play time to work through their stress and fears. They may act out scenes with toys. Bath time is also a common setting to play through frustrations. When they play, stay on the sidelines, listen, and observe. Let them play without interruptions. As long as they aren't hurting anyone, this is usually a good way for kids to express themselves and process their feelings. You can also use your observations to guide future conversations.

3. **Get support.** For children struggling with fear after divorce or separation, DivorceCare for Kids can be a game changer in how they process their worries and anxieties. It is a group support program that helps children understand that they are not alone and there are others who care about them. It gives them tools to deal with fears and provides a place where they can also help other children. Find out more about this program at **dc4k.org**.

# DIVORCE Care®

## *Living* FORWARD
### A GUIDED JOURNAL

## A guided journal for healing and direction

**Continue healing and prepare for your future**

Not sure about what lies ahead after your divorce or separation? This textured, hardcover journal can help you make sense of your emotions and make wise decisions for your future.

**Go deeper in your healing with the *Living Forward* journal.**

*"When I lay it all out on paper, I can see things clearer."*

Order your journal today: **divorcecare.org/journal**

# FAMILY & *Friends*

## *Navigating changes in relationships*

Divorce changes more than your marriage. You're relearning how to interact with people as a single person—including friends, your in-laws, perhaps even the barista at the coffee shop you and your ex went to together.

Filled to the brim with emotions, this is no easy task. As you spend time this week with the **video**, the daily **On My Own** exercises, and **My Weekly Journal**, you'll gain new insight into how to relate to your family and friends now that you're divorced or separated. You'll learn:

- **How to emotionally detach from your former spouse**
- **How to decide if you should include your former in-laws in your life**
- **How you and your former spouse can co-parent**
- **How to ease your friends' discomfort around you**

# VIDEO OUTLINE

Use this outline to write down important concepts, encouraging words, or questions you may have while viewing the video.

## RELATING TO YOUR EX-SPOUSE

Detaching emotionally

## CO-PARENTING

Separate personal and parental issues

Allow time with both parents

Keep the peace in front of the children

Keep the kids' routines consistent

Keep lines of communication open

Recognize the effects on adult children

## RELATING TO FORMER IN-LAWS

Recognize the possible challenges

Tell them you want a relationship

Don't talk about the past failures

## RELATING TO YOUR FRIENDS

Accept that friendships can change

> *"Two are better than one. …*
> *If either of them falls down,*
> *one can help the other up.*
> *But pity anyone who falls and has*
> *no one to help them up."*
>
> **Ecclesiastes 4:9–10**

Be patient with them

Avoid "mind reading"

## CHANGING FRIENDSHIPS

### Additional help

I'm emotionally attached to my ex — p. 64

Beware of gossip — p. 65

I want revenge — p. 66

# ON MY *Own*

## Wisdom and encouragement for your new journey

### CHE-VON'S STORY

*"My daughters experience a lot of sadness. They're very confused about things and have inner turmoil regarding their relationship with their father. And I'm the one who has to make sure homework gets done, that they're being respectful to their teachers, and that they're not on social media '27 hours a day.' Dad is able to show up and be the Disney World father. It's very conflicting and very stressful."* This week, you'll learn how to handle challenges in your relationships.

## 1 — I'M EMOTIONALLY ATTACHED TO MY EX

It's common for your thoughts and emotions to continually stray to your ex: *Despite everything, I still love him. … We were planning to travel once the kids were out of the house. … She's so self-absorbed; I can't stand it.* But remaining emotionally attached to your former spouse can hurt you and keep you from fully healing. Ron L. Deal shares steps you can take to begin separating yourself emotionally, or, as he calls it, "decoupling":

### STEP 1: REDUCE the time you spend thinking or talking about …

- Shattered dreams and plans

- Your ex's flaws

- Bad things that could happen to your former spouse

- The rejection of divorce

- Expectations that your ex will assist you (other than parenting)

It's hard to simply stop thinking those thoughts. You need to replace them with other things. Over the next few months, replace Step 1 thoughts with Step 2 activities.

### STEP 2: REPLACE those thoughts with these activities (pick 1–2 changes at a time):

- Remove painful reminders of your former spouse from your home

- Respect your former spouse's privacy

- Learn a skill that you currently depend on your ex to provide (to help you become less reliant on him or her)

- Build or deepen nonromantic friendships (this often begins with pursuing a common interest and then grows into supporting/ helping one another)

- Confess and ask forgiveness for wrongs against your former spouse (you could do this in writing, face-to-face, or with a phone call)

- Devote more time to Bible reading, church activities, and prayer (grow closer to God!)

**Tip:** If you're not divorced, be cautious about emotionally detaching prematurely. Depending upon your situation, it may be wise to remain open to reconciliation for a season.

## 2  I WANT TO GIVE MY EX A PIECE OF MY MIND!

If you plant an apple tree, you expect to get apples, right? Proverbs 18:21 talks about the kind of "fruit" you're planting every time you open your mouth. Every word you say is a seed you're planting, and something's going to grow from it. The verse says: "The tongue has the power of life and death, and those who love it will eat its fruit [reap its consequences]."

When your ex pushes your buttons, it's easy to let loose with the first response that comes to mind. But you can save yourself so much pain if you follow the advice of these Proverbs instead.

### GOD'S MESSAGE TO YOU

*"Too much talk leads to sin. Be sensible and keep your mouth shut."* (Proverbs 10:19 NLT)

*"Those who guard their lips preserve [protect] their lives, but those who speak rashly will come to ruin."* (Proverbs 13:3)

1. **Describe a time when the outcome would have turned out better if you had said nothing at all. How was what you said tied to the negative outcome?**

2. **According to today's verses, what can happen when you speak before thinking?**

3. **What kind of reminder could you use to help you control your tongue?**

### REMEMBER

- When you can't think of something helpful or uplifting to say in the moment, it's better to keep your mouth shut.

- If you want healthy, nourishing fruit to grow, you've got to plant good seeds. Consider what you've been planting with your words. Because that's what will grow.

## 3  BEWARE OF GOSSIP

### IT'S A TEMPTING TRAP

*"You won't* believe *what I saw my ex doing. ..."*

When you've been hurt, it's so tempting to gossip! And when someone else wants to share gossip with you, it's tempting to listen. In fact, Proverbs 26:22

describes the words of a gossip as "choice morsels" (bits you want to gobble up).

Whether you're on the sharing or receiving end, gossip easily entangles everyone. God disapproves of gossip because it strains relationships, damages people's reputations, and nurtures a negative attitude in us.

Gossip also feeds bitterness. After her divorce, Elsa learned this lesson firsthand: "My conversations with my coworkers were not very good. I would get off the phone after an angry conversation with my ex, and I would just sit and beat up on him."

An important part of moving forward in your divorce recovery is avoiding this snare.

## IT'S EASY TO OVERLOOK

How do you know if you're gossiping? Gossip is sharing negative information about someone that the recipient doesn't have a good reason to know. So, if you're sharing negative information with others who aren't part of the problem you're facing, nor legitimately part of the solution you're seeking, then you're gossiping. Gossip is also *listening* to negative information about someone that you don't have a good reason to know.

Take a few moments to consider:

- How often do you share or receive negative information about others?

- What steps can you take to avoid sharing or listening to gossip?

## 4 I WANT REVENGE

It's a knee-jerk reaction. When someone hurts you, you probably want to hurt that person back. Yes, it's a natural tendency, but it's not healthy to act on it. Dealing with angry words, gossip, and lies with more of the same will only bring added pain and complications into your life.

To protect you from this pain, God has some instructions for you.

## GOD'S MESSAGE TO YOU

*"9 Don't repay evil for evil. Don't retaliate with insults when people insult you. Instead, pay them back with a blessing. That is what God has called you to do, and he will grant you his blessing. 10 For the Scriptures say, 'If you want to enjoy life and see many happy days, keep your tongue from speaking evil and your lips from telling lies. 11 Turn away from evil and do good. Search for peace, and work to maintain it.'"*
(1 Peter 3:9–11 NLT)

1. **How do you respond when someone treats you badly? What happens when you respond this way?**

2. **It's not easy to just "stop" doing a behavior. Here God tells us to replace harmful behaviors with helpful ones. What positive actions should you choose? Why?**

## REMEMBER

- Just because someone throws something at you, you don't need to throw it back—or even catch it, for that matter.

- Saying something encouraging to the other person is one way to pursue peace.

- God's presence and forgiveness in your life can make it possible to respond to bad actions with good ones, allowing you to receive even more blessings.

*"You'll never regret taking the high road."* – Vaneetha

# 5 I WANT MY WORDS TO HEAL, NOT HURT

When someone is frustrating you, it can be hard to think of anything positive to say. But don't underestimate the potential of your words.

## GOD'S MESSAGE TO YOU

*"Do not let any unwholesome talk come out of your mouths, but only what is helpful for building others up according to their needs, that it may benefit those who listen."* (Ephesians 4:29)

*"1 Remind the people … to be ready to do whatever is good, 2 to slander no one, to be peaceable and considerate, and always to be gentle toward everyone."* (Titus 3:1–2)

1. **According to Ephesians 4:29, what do your words have the potential to do for others?**

2. **How can you figure out what words would help build up others—before you speak?**

3. **Picture yourself putting these verses into practice. Which of your relationships would be the most likely to benefit from this change?**

## REMEMBER

- Think about how the words of others affect you (in both good ways and bad).

- Other people's negative words don't have to guide your responses.

- Many people think it's okay to say negative things when the other person "deserves it." In reality, none of us get things right every time; we're not always "nice" or deserving of good ourselves.

**BRIGHTER DAYS**

## CHE-VON'S STORY

*"What I've learned is no matter what you feel, try not to speak negatively about your children's [other parent]. Kids need to have a good perception of their parents. And it needs to be because of what they've observed, not based off of what you're saying. Allow them to see with their own eyes and make their own judgments about their parents. As a co-parent, you just have to trust God to guide you and give you the words. And every single day God gives me the strength for that day."*

## NEXT SESSION

Tackling your financial and legal concerns.

# MY WEEKLY Journal

When relationships get messy or uncomfortable, use your journal to think through how you might respond in a productive way. You can use the following statements to help in this process. Use them to come up with a wise plan, whenever you are facing a struggle in a relationship.

**1. I'm finding it difficult to be around …**

**2. When I am around …, I usually …**

**3. Most times, the outcome is …**

**4. These situations could be better if I …**

As you consider #4, the following verses can help:

- 1 Peter 2:1
- Proverbs 18:21
- Proverbs 11:13
- Proverbs 26:20–22

## CHART YOUR PROGRESS

Place a check in the boxes to identify how you are feeling in each area this week: emotionally, physically, etc. Even better? Substitute a word or two to describe how you are doing.

|  | REALLY BAD | OKAY | PRETTY GOOD | GREAT |
|---|---|---|---|---|
| **Emotionally** | | | | |
| **Physically** | | | | |
| **Spiritually** (closeness to God) | | | | |
| **Relationally** (closeness to others) | | | | |
| **How your life is in general** | | | | |

# How will divorce affect my kids?
## (And how can I help them?)

You're going through a lot—and so are your kids. Here are three common struggles kids face and helpful strategies to work through them.

## 1. They wrestle with emotions

Like you, your kids will experience a full range of emotions in response to your divorce. You can expect to see anger, sadness, frustration, longing, and stress. Some children become unruly and cause problems at school. They may have difficulty concentrating, and their school performance might be affected. Other effects are trouble sleeping, changes in appetite, and regressive behavior (e.g., young children may have bed-wetting accidents).

Here are actions you could take:

- Let your child talk to a counselor.

- Talk to your child's teacher and child care provider. Ask for their input.

- For a teen, enlist other people to encourage and spend time with your child.

- Register your elementary age child into a DC4K (DivorceCare for Kids) group.

- Purchase books about divorce to read together. One good book is *Stories for Kids in Divorce* by Linda Jacobs, which includes questions to stimulate conversations between you and your child.

## 2. They misunderstand

Ron L. Deal says, "Children are good observers of their world, but they're poor interpreters." **It's common for kids to blame themselves for the divorce and feel insecure** in their relationships.

Here's what you can do about it: Show them **physical affection** and tell them you love them. And **explain that the divorce is not their fault**. It also helps for you to keep things calm at your place, especially when the children are transitioning between homes.

## 3. They don't communicate

In an effort to protect their children, many parents hide their struggles from the kids. As a result, **the kids think they are supposed to hide their feelings too.**

**Model for them that it's okay to talk about their feelings.** You could say things like, "I'm sad," "I'm lonely," or "I'm embarrassed when I go places because I wonder what people are thinking."

Try sitting down each week and saying, "Tell me two good things that happened this week and one thing you had a hard time with. I'll go first."

Another great idea for tweens and teens is to develop a back-and-forth journal. The kid writes his or her issues or questions in the journal in the evening and places it in a designated spot. Then you read it in the morning and leave a short note for your tween or teen; it's also a great place to compliment your child.

## Don't try to do it alone!

From diapers to dentist appointments to school dances, **there's a lot to juggle at any stage of parenting**. And now you have to figure out how to do this as a divorced single parent. It can be tough on everyone. That's why you need a support system. It doesn't need to be a large group, but you need a small circle of people you can count on. They can help with after-school events, soccer games, and anything else you think is necessary.

It will take courage and humility to ask for this help, but it's crucial for your kids.

# How to watch
## session videos online

Log on to **divorcecare.org/my** to watch full DivorceCare session videos. It's a great option if you:

- Missed a meeting and want to see the video
- Want to rewatch something you saw
- Want to review before your group meeting

## Watch the videos today!

---

# DIVORCE *Care*.
# Surviving
# the Holidays

Thanksgiving and Christmas can be very painful when you are separated or divorced. We want to help you survive, and even enjoy, the next holiday season.

### Seminar

The Surviving the Holidays event features an encouraging video session and group discussion.

### Online help

Find articles and videos that will equip you to survive the approaching holidays.

"Only Surviving the Holidays could have prepared me for the emotions that ambushed me."

# Financial
# & LEGAL ISSUES

*Resources to resolve your concerns*

Attorneys. Bills. Child support. You may be entering unfamiliar territory. On top of that, the accounting and "legalese" involved can be pretty intimidating.

This week the **video**, **On My Own** exercises, and **My Weekly Journal** will provide clear, easy-to-follow guides to help you understand these issues and take steps to protect yourself legally and financially. You'll discover:

- **How to regain your financial footing**
- **How to avoid common legal mistakes**
- **How to think biblically about debt**

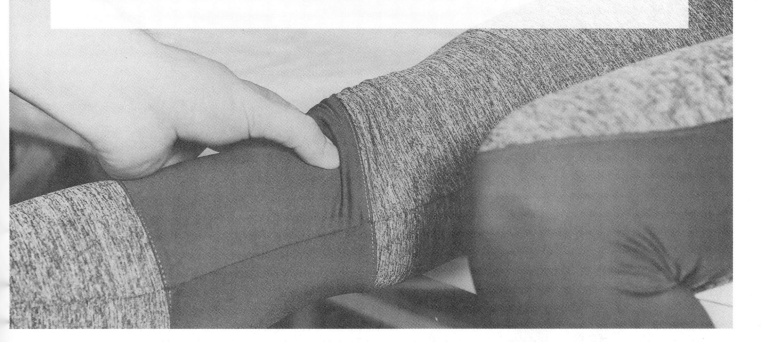

# VIDEO OUTLINE

Use this outline to write down important concepts, encouraging words, or questions you may have while viewing the video.

## UNHELPFUL REACTIONS

## ASSESS YOUR CONDITION

An immediate adjustment in spending is required

## START WITH SMALL STEPS

**STEP 1:** Begin an emergency fund

**STEP 2:** Get out of debt

**STEP 3:** Increase your emergency fund

## COMMIT TO A BUDGET

Divide income across monthly expenses

Adjust the plan as needed

> *"A budget is people telling their money what to do instead of wondering where it went."*
>
> **Dave Ramsey**

Stick to the plan faithfully

*"You sacrifice. You work a lot of hours. You don't vacation. You don't eat out. You do the consignment sale [for] clothes."*

**Dave Ramsey**

Don't hesitate to ask for help

*"Plans fail for lack of counsel, but with many advisers they succeed."*

**Proverbs 15:22**

## A ROLE FOR BANKRUPTCY

## ACCESSING SUPPORT

Child or spousal support

Other types of support

- Medicaid
- Food stamps
- Your church
- Food banks
- Child care vouchers

*"So in everything, do to others what you would have them do to you."*

**Matthew 7:12a**

## FACING LEGAL PROBLEMS

Pursue a fair distribution of assets

Don't use the law for revenge

### *Additional help*


**Financial freedom** — **p. 74**

**Top 4 legal mistakes** — **p. 75**

**Bankruptcy: Is it a good option?** — **p. 77**

# ON MY *Own*

## Wisdom and encouragement for your new journey

### ALISA'S STORY

*"My credit was bad, I had no money, and I didn't know if I was going to be able to get a car. I had the car my husband had purchased [while we were still married]. It was in his name because I wasn't working. After the breakup, he said he wanted the car back—and he stopped paying. That blew me away. I was like, 'If you take this car, how am I going to get to work?' I worked 25 miles one way. I didn't know what I was going to do. So I started praying."* If you, like Alisa, have financial or legal worries, this week's exercises will help.

## 1 · FINANCIAL FREEDOM ... HERE I COME!

What's the key to financial freedom? Having a budget. Don't worry—it's easier than you might think.

To create a personal budget, you start by tracking your spending for one month (keep track of every dollar that goes out: groceries, rent, insurance, eating out, etc.). The more detailed you are, the better. After that, you'll figure out where you're spending more than you're bringing in, and you can make adjustments. These tips will help you track your spending:

- **Take advantage of online banking** – When you use your debit card for purchases, you can check your online bank account for a detailed list of your spending.

- **Check your bank statements** – Use your monthly bank statements as a way to help track your spending. (Pay with your debit card instead of checks or cash, because the checks might not show up on the statement right away and you might not remember what you spent the cash on.)

- **Keep receipts** – Identify a place in your wallet, purse, or drawer, on your phone, etc., where you'll keep your receipts for a month. At the month's end, you can easily see how you've spent your money.

### GET STARTED

Use the budget worksheet in the back of this book to start your detailed budget (or download the interactive spreadsheet). See page 137.

*"I had a friend who did a budget sheet with me. Afterward, I said, 'Okay, I can do this.'"* – Theresa

## 2 DO WE HAVE TO LET THE ATTORNEYS FIGHT IT OUT?

Often divorce, custody, support, and property division get settled in a courtroom by attorneys and judges (this is called litigation). But did you know other options are available?

### SETTLEMENT AGREEMENT

A settlement agreement (also called a separation agreement, domestic contract, postnuptial agreement, and parenting agreement) is a private contract between the parties and, once signed and notarized, is a legally binding contract enforceable by law.

Agreements are voluntary and require your consent before signing. They are more cost-efficient than other methods, and they give you the flexibility to handle only one or two issues (e.g., only property, or only custody and child support). They also allow you to work with the church or counselors if you want to include accountability or morality clauses (which are prohibited in a courtroom).

### MEDIATION

If you and your spouse can't engage directly in a healthy way, a mediator can act as a neutral third party to lay out the issues of divorce, property settlement, custody, etc., and help you come to an agreement. Using a mediator can keep things more civil than litigation and can give you more control over the outcomes. Mediation can be completed in one day; litigation can last up to two years.

### ARBITRATION

Arbitration is also cheaper and faster than litigation. This is basically the court process in a private setting. You and your spouse each present your case, then the arbitrator makes a decision similar to a judge. With binding arbitration, the decision is legally binding. With non-binding arbitration, you can decide whether to submit to the decision. Non-binding arbitration basically gives you a test run to see what a judge might say about your case.

### WHAT ARE YOUR OPTIONS?

Regulations about mediation and arbitration vary depending on where you live. If you'd like to learn more about your options, contact your local courthouse or an attorney to ask about the possibility of mediation or arbitration in the context of a divorce.

*"Sometimes you need a steady hand on a swerving car."* – Keith Battle

## 3 WATCH OUT FOR THESE TOP 4 LEGAL MISTAKES

The situation is overwhelming. The legal aspects are confusing. It's easy to make mistakes when you're involved in divorce disputes. Here are four common legal blunders that family law attorney Tiffany Lesnik says to avoid.

1. **Choosing the wrong attorney**

   Shop around. Get a second or third opinion before you spend thousands of dollars and make life-impacting legal decisions. **Be sure to choose someone you feel comfortable with and trust.** Expect your case to take 10 hours of prep time for every hour of scheduled court time. Multiply that by the attorney's hourly rate to get an idea of your total fees.

2. **Leaving the residence**

   "In most [jurisdictions], if you leave the marital residence, you may not be able to return," explains

Lesnik. "So it's very important that before you leave, you collect anything of value—birth certificates, social security cards, medications, heirlooms. **Anything you don't want to lose, make sure you take that with you before you go.**" Keep in mind, the residence and possessions will be subject to equitable division later.

### 3. Posting before thinking

Keep in mind that anything you post, text, or otherwise share can be printed out and used against you in court. **Before you hit "Send," consider whether you would want a judge to see what you wrote.** And remember, your kids might see it too—would you want them to read that?

### 4. Signing blindly

You might want things finished so badly that you'll sign anything to be done. But many documents are final. It won't matter if you didn't understand what you were signing, didn't read it, or didn't have an attorney. **Make sure you understand any paperwork before you sign.** Have someone else review anything you plan to sign; you could be signing away significant rights or assets.

## 4 IF I ONLY HAD A TREASURE MAP …

Bills are due. The kids need clothes. The car is making a noise that can't be good. Life would be easier if you had a few extra bucks.

When you're struggling to make ends meet, it's hard not to focus on money. And you should put some focus there. But your attitude toward money is more important than how much of it you have.

## GOD'S MESSAGE TO YOU

*"Don't love money; be satisfied with what you have. For God has said, 'I will never fail you. I will never abandon you.'"* (Hebrews 13:5 NLT)

*"11 For I have learned to be content whatever the circumstances. 12 I know what it is to be in need, and I know what it is to have plenty. I have learned the secret*

*of being content in any and every situation, whether well fed or hungry, whether living in plenty or in want. 13 I can do all this through him who gives me strength."* (Philippians 4:11b–13)

1. **Fill in the blanks: "I would be content if I had**

   _____ **dollars or a new** _____**."**

2. **Can you be content if you don't have these things? Explain why.**

3. **According to today's verses, what are the secrets to contentment? Why?**

4. **What are the benefits of knowing contentment is something that can be "learned"?**

## REMEMBER

- Money is helpful to have, but everything actually belongs to God, and He is the one who ultimately provides.

- Proverbs 30:8b offers this prayer: "Give me neither poverty nor riches, but give me only my daily bread."

*"This is an opportunity to analyze what's really important."* – Travis Sasser

# 5 BANKRUPTCY: IS IT A GOOD OPTION?

Bankruptcy carries financial, social, and even spiritual weight. But sometimes it may seem the only option. Bankruptcy attorney Travis Sasser answers these common questions:

**Q: I'm considering bankruptcy. What options do I have?**

A: Realistically consider the resources you have to address the debt. Bankruptcy could be a good option, but it's not the only option. You might be able to avoid bankruptcy through:

- **Settlements:** Settle with your creditors for a lump sum or reduced amount.
- **Debt management:** Get extended repayment terms through a debt management plan offered by a credit counseling service.

Be sure to discuss your options with godly people you respect.

**Q: Can bankruptcy be part of a God-honoring strategy to handle debt?**

A: After divorce, resources may be limited. Bankruptcy *can* be a responsible way to address debt, if two key things are in place: (1) This should not be a way to maintain an inappropriate lifestyle (overspending, gambling, etc.). (2) You are honest about reporting your resources (your assets and income).

**Q: Is declaring bankruptcy a sign of personal failure or sin?**

A: It's understandable there may be some shame because of choices that were made, but filing bankruptcy is not inherently sinful. Now, if somebody is unwilling to make reasonable sacrifices to pay debt, that would be concerning. But that's not true for the majority of people considering bankruptcy. In many instances, they had every intention to pay, and intervening circumstances resulted in financial distress. And now they need grace when they fall short.

## BRIGHTER DAYS

# ALISA'S STORY

*"I've had to learn to rely on God and trust Him. He worked everything out. My daughter was able to bless me with a down payment for a car that I could afford. In the interim, I found out my coworker lives right down the street, and she took me to work until I got the car.*

*"I had to get smarter and wiser about my finances. I started doing a little extra part-time job, and I asked God to show me how to handle my finances and pay off my debts. And He's done that. Since I've been on my own, I've built up my credit, paid off some debt, and got a decent car."*

## NEXT SESSION

Strategies for resolving conflict in difficult relationships.

# MY WEEKLY Journal

Is your mind spinning with legal and financial worries? Sort through some of these thoughts in your journal this week. Getting your concerns out of your mind and on paper can help. Use these statements to get started:

1. **My biggest financial and legal concerns right now are …**

2. **I'm handling those concerns by …**

3. **So far, my actions have led to …**

4. **A next step that I learned from the video and On My Own exercises to improve these situations is …**

## CHART YOUR PROGRESS

Place a check in the boxes to identify how you are feeling in each area this week: emotionally, physically, etc. Even better? Substitute a word or two to describe how you are doing.

|  | REALLY BAD | OKAY | PRETTY GOOD | GREAT |
|---|---|---|---|---|
| **Emotionally** |  |  |  |  |
| **Physically** |  |  |  |  |
| **Spiritually** (closeness to God) |  |  |  |  |
| **Relationally** (closeness to others) |  |  |  |  |
| **How your life is in general** |  |  |  |  |

# Parents

## *I'm worried about my child's safety in my ex's home*

Sometimes children will say or do something that causes you to question whether they are safe at your former spouse's home. Pay attention to your children to determine if their physical safety is at risk. Some children may be unhappy, but they are not in danger.

Children are considered to be in danger if they suffer some form of abuse or neglect. This could involve a child who is beaten, burned, molested or touched inappropriately, locked in a closet, abandoned, or not fed.

Family law attorney Tiffany Lesnik outlines some actions you might consider, with the guidance of a professional who has experience handling these issues.*

### 1. Question carefully

- Be careful not to influence your child's testimony. Ask an open-ended question, such as "What happened?" Then let your child talk freely. Follow up with questions such as "What did you think about that?" (Be careful asking kids how they "felt" about it. Your kids still love the other parent, and they don't want to betray that parent.)

- Sometimes it's better to observe your child's play than to question a child. You know your child and what is normal. When you see play or activity that is not normal, document it.

- If it's something severe, like inappropriate touching, many children will tell the story only once. You don't want that one time to be to you, but to someone of authority, such as a child abuse counselor, police officer, or pediatrican.

Document what your child shares with you. Include the date and time you talked. Use ink, or document on a computer that displays the time and date. Never record your assumptions or feelings about what happened with the other parent. Only document what your child said or did.

### 2. Take your child to the doctor

- If you're worried about suspicious bruises or marks, ask a doctor for an examination.

- Document suspected abuse with photos and a written doctor's report. Do not take a picture of any private areas. Don't post on social media. If there is a vindictive former partner, the photos could be used against you.

### 3. Get a therapist or child development expert involved

- This neutral third party provides someone for the child to confide in.

- The child development expert or therapist will know when it is appropriate to contact Child Protective Services. (Be cautious, as Child Protective Services are able to remove children from a home.)

### 4. Ask for a welfare check

- If you're concerned your child may be abandoned or otherwise in danger, the police can do what is known as a "welfare check."

### 5. File a protective order

- If there is a serious issue with abuse or neglect, you can file a domestic violence protective order (also called a restraining order).

### 6. File for emergency custody

- When abuse is suspected, you may file for emergency custody. Situations that qualify for emergency custody typically include sexual abuse, "substantial" bodily injury (something that leaves marks or could permanently injure a child), exposure to substance abuse, or neglect of a child's basic needs.

Be sure your emotions are not getting in the way of you being fair. While some parents hate to admit it, they really don't want their children to enjoy going to the other parent's home. Be wise about any actions you take that involve your children.

*\* These options apply in the United States. If you're in another country, you'll need to find out what options are available in your area.*

# ARE YOU FULLY PREPARED FOR *Court?*

The thought of going to court can be overwhelming. You might fear the conflict it could cause. *(Why rehash hurts from the past?)* Or you might wonder how going to court fits with Jesus' teaching on peace and "turning the other cheek." *(Can I go to court and still honor the Lord?)*

To help with these struggles, check out the following insights from DivorceCare experts.

## FACING THE FEAR

Attorney Tiffany Lesnik says: "The decisions judges make have an enormous impact on people's lives. However, if you're so intimidated by the legal system that you refuse to engage, that's a problem. If someone initiates a lawsuit and you refuse to respond, they could have a hearing without you. That might mean your ex-spouse gets 100% custody, or you get no alimony, or your ex-spouse gets the house or retirement account. You have to at least show up. The other possibility is that your case will get dismissed. Again that could mean no child support, no alimony, no property."

## TURNING THE OTHER CHEEK

Jesus tells us to turn the other cheek (Matthew 5:39). Does that mean you can't go to court or that you have to give in on every issue?

Ken Sande of Peacemaker Ministries says no. "Primarily what the ['turn the other cheek'] passage means in a divorce is that you don't let personal offenses guide you. If you feel intense emotions, take a break, pray about it, talk to somebody else." Don't go in there angry, fighting for every dollar out of spite. Stay focused on the more important issues: the relationship you have with your children and the way you treat your ex.

Dr. Stephen Viars adds, "If you know a divorce is inevitable, there's absolutely nothing wrong with saying, 'I am going to stand up for the proper amount of child support so my children's needs are properly met.' That's not sinful; that's stewardship [responsible management of what's entrusted to your care]. And there's absolutely nothing wrong in securing one's rightful share of the retirement funds, the business, or [other] assets."

## WORKING WITH AN ANGRY EX-SPOUSE

Jesus taught, "Blessed are the peacemakers, for they will be called children of God" (Matthew 5:9). Ken Sande offers some clarification: "It's important to say up front that being a peacemaker does not mean you just give in on significant issues when someone disagrees with you. (Jesus didn't do that!)

"One of the passages I use when I'm trying to be a peacemaker is Romans 12:18. Paul says, 'If it is possible, as far as it depends on you, live at peace with [everyone].' Paul recognizes that sometimes you have to be prepared for unavoidable conflict. But there may be a way to 'live at peace' with your former spouse if you exercise control over your attitude, your words, and the timing of your conversation."

How? Well, you may be in a legal battle, but you can choose to communicate in a loving and gentle way.

"Don't think of a disagreement as a tug-of-war *(I'm going to win and that means you lose!)*," Sande explains. "Instead, try to have a conversation where both of you can walk away feeling like it's been helpful. This has more to do with your attitude than anything else."

# CONTINUE HEALING WITH

## My DivorceCare+

### YOUR PERSONAL LIBRARY OF DIVORCECARE VIDEOS

**$25** annual subscription

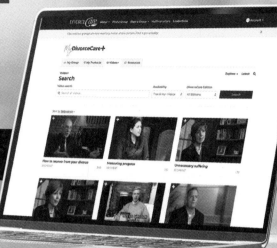

# What is MyDivorceCare+?

MyDivorceCare+ is a library of hundreds of additional divorce recovery videos designed to help you continue healing during your DivorceCare group and after it ends.

**With this annual subscription service, you can:**

- Access 200+ videos essential to your healing
- Get more advice from popular DivorceCare experts & testimonials
- Find answers to the questions you are struggling with
- Learn more about your divorce recovery by watching previous editions of DivorceCare

**Get continued support after your group sessions end—subscribe today!**

## NEW CONTENT ADDED MONTHLY

## Subscribe or learn more at

### DIVORCECARE.ORG/PLUS

# Conflict

## *Dealing with disagreements*

*What am I supposed to say to THAT?*

Dealing with challenging people (and people in general) involves conflict—it's unavoidable. So how can you handle it in a healthy way?

This week's **video**, **On My Own** exercises, and **My Weekly Journal** will help you figure out what to do when you're pushed to your limits. You'll learn:

- **How to plan well for difficult conversations**
- **How to listen well in difficult conversations**
- **How to respond well in difficult conversations**

# VIDEO OUTLINE

Use this outline to write down important concepts, encouraging words, or questions you may have while viewing the video.

## HANDLING YOUR ANGER

Choose to be a peacemaker

Become more self-aware

Plan out your moves before the conversation

Stay focused on one issue at a time

Choose your words carefully

Seek common ground with the other person

Learn the "backstory" for the other viewpoint

Become aware of body language

Involve the other person

> "Not looking to your own interests
> but each of you to
> the interests of the others."
>
> **Philippians 2:4**

## WHEN OTHERS ARE ANGRY

Respond with a "gentle answer"

> "A gentle answer
> turns away wrath, but
> a harsh word stirs up anger."
>
> **Proverbs 15:1**

Wait until everyone is calm

Make honoring God your top priority

### Additional help

How to communicate ——————— p. 86

Did I really just say that? ——————— p. 87

I want to make them pay ——————— p. 87

# ON MY *Own*

## Wisdom and encouragement for your new journey

### JONATHON'S STORY

*"[While co-parenting] I get a lot of pushback. And it's not because she really feels something would be bad for the children—it feels like she just wants to contradict me. If I want to go left, she says, 'No, you should go right.' It's challenging because ideally we'd be able to keep the focus on the children and then leave it at that. But we tend to disagree on a lot of things."* Do you feel like there are more disagreements than agreements with your former spouse? This week you'll develop better ways to interact with difficult people in your life.

## 1 HOW TO COMMUNICATE WITH A MANIPULATOR

Conversations with manipulative people can leave your head spinning. How is it possible to communicate with this type of person?

Dr. John Applegate points out that people who use manipulation are trying to exert control over you, to direct you and the conversation where they want to go. Taking things in a different direction requires planning ahead. Here are 5 ways experts recommend to prepare.

1. **Be humble:** When you're humble, you get offended less easily, and you don't feel the need to defend yourself. Consider what things cause you to be reactive or defensive, and practice being in that situation while maintaining a humble and respectful attitude.

2. **Set boundaries:** Decide for yourself ahead of time where the conversation is allowed to go (topics and time length), then stick to those boundaries.

3. **Say no:** There are times when you need to say no, but not out of anger. Be prepared to say no diplomatically, but firmly.

4. **Watch for misdirects:** Common manipulation tactics include bringing up old arguments and using the words "always" and "never." Recognize these for what they are and don't play into them.

5. **Press pause:** If the person is unable to respond to redirections, you may need to tell him or her that you can't have this conversation right now, then suggest a time to pick it up in a few hours or days.

## WRITE IT OUT

In some situations a conversation might not be ideal. Dr. Erikka Dzirasa suggests writing a letter or email. Include:

- A short list of things you need to agree on

- Possible solutions

- "Which ones work for you?"

- "Here are the ones I prefer."

## 2 DID I REALLY JUST SAY THAT?

*I did it again! In my frustration, I said some terrible things that could affect this relationship forever. I wish I could turn back the clock and change my reaction.*

Your words have power. They can hurt, and they can heal, taking your life in different directions. That's why it's important to think carefully before you speak, especially in the heat of an argument (even though that can be really hard to do!).

## GOD'S MESSAGE TO YOU

*"The words of the reckless pierce like swords, but the tongue of the wise brings healing."* (Proverbs 12:18)

*"Gracious words are a honeycomb, sweet to the soul and healing to the bones."* (Proverbs 16:24)

*"The wicked put up a bold front, but the upright give thought to their ways."* (Proverbs 21:29)

1. **In the middle of a disagreement, how carefully do you consider your words before you speak? Think of one or two of your closest relationships and describe your track record in this.**

2. **How does your track record compare with the counsel from these proverbs?**

3. **According to today's verses, what can happen if you give thought to your response and speak calmly and lovingly instead?**

## REMEMBER

- The words you speak can change your relationships and your life—in positive or negative ways.

- By making a commitment to think before you speak, you can spare yourself and others unnecessary hurt. Even if you fail at times, it's worth returning to this commitment again and again.

*"I told God, I'm done. I can't fight any more."*
– Vickilynn

## 3 I WANT TO MAKE THEM PAY

Many of today's blockbuster films are about revenge. Viewers cheer on the heroes as they track down the "bad guys" who did people wrong and take them out. When people hurt you, you may want to react in the same way. But this isn't the plotline God wants for your life. He has something better for you in mind.

## GOD'S MESSAGE TO YOU

*"Bless those who persecute [mistreat] you; bless and do not curse."* (Romans 12:14)

*"**17** Do not repay anyone evil for evil. Be careful to do what is right in the eyes of everyone. **18** If it is possible, as far as it depends on you, live at peace with everyone."* (Romans 12:17–18)

1. **When you are mistreated, which of these statements best describes your typical response?**

   ☐ I think about what I could do *for* that person.

   ☐ I think about what I could do *to* that person.

2. **How well can you control other people's actions? According to Romans 12:18, whose actions are you responsible for?**

3. **If you followed the responses in today's verses, what would be the resulting impact? (On you? On others?)**

## REMEMBER

- You can't control what others do, but you can always control your own response.

- The next time someone is angry at you, think about how you can respond in a way that encourages peace.

*"God's in control, and He knows what's going on at the other house."* – Jonathon

## I'M GOOD AT HANDLING CONFLICT ... I THINK

Maybe you think you handle conflict pretty well. And you may be right, for the most part. But this assumption can lead you to blame other people for starting and escalating conflicts—and leave you blind to the fact that you might be contributing to the drama as well.

## GOD'S MESSAGE TO YOU

*"13 Who is wise and understanding among you? Let them show it … by deeds done in the humility that comes from wisdom. 14 But if you harbor bitter envy and selfish ambition in your hearts, … 15 such 'wisdom' does not come down from heaven. … 16 There you find disorder and every evil practice.*

*"17 But the wisdom that comes from heaven is first of all pure; then peace-loving, considerate, submissive, full of mercy and good fruit, impartial and sincere."* (James 3:13–17)

1. **Describe what a typical conflict with your former spouse looks like.**

2. **According to today's verses, what does the person look like who is wise in the midst of conflict? What words describe someone who is NOT wise?**

3. **Based on your answer to #2, are you relying on godly wisdom to handle conflict and promote peace? What would be at least one change you could make?**

## REMEMBER

- It's important to assess: "Are my choices based on God's wisdom, or my own?"

- In order to promote peace in your relationship with your ex, let your words and actions be directed by God's wisdom.

*"The more I tried to take things into my own hands, the worse things got."* – Jonathon

# 5 THE OTHER SIDE OF CONVERSATION

People often have blind spots when it comes to assessing their listening skills. So how do you become aware of your blind spots? One way is to periodically ask one or two close friends, or a family member, how you're doing as a listener. Another way is to use God's Word, the Bible. As you read today's verses, ask yourself, "How well do I do that?"

## GOD'S MESSAGE TO YOU

*"Fools find no pleasure in understanding but delight in airing their own opinions."* (Proverbs 18:2)

*"To answer before listening—that is folly and shame."* (Proverbs 18:13)

*"The heart of the discerning acquires knowledge, for the ears of the wise seek it out."* (Proverbs 18:15)

1. **On a scale from 1 (very bad) to 10 (very good), how would rate your listening habits? (Also ask your friends and see what they say.)**

   1   2   3   4   5   6   7   8   9   10

2. **Why would "answering before listening" be foolish and shameful? When have you experienced this?**

3. **If the "ears of the wise" seek out knowledge, what does that suggest you should do in most conversations?**

## REMEMBER

- Good listening requires self-control.

- Good listening requires a willingness to put others' concerns ahead of your own.

- Good listening will be important for receiving assistance, resolving conflicts, and building friendships.

## JONATHON'S STORY

*"I've come to grips with the fact that I can't control what she does. Just thinking ahead helps me deal with my anger: This is how she is. It is what it is. I don't have to respond, especially not in front of the kids. The best thing for me to do is breathe, pause, and think back to what I've said in the past that wasn't glorifying Christ or uplifting anybody—and remember how that turned out. And replace it with something positive."*

## NEXT SESSION

**Forgiveness can transform your life.**

# MY WEEKLY Journal

It's hard to hold your tongue when conversations get SO frustrating! Use your journaling time to express your frustrations in a safe and healthy way. Here are some prompts to help:

**1. I recently experienced conflict when …**

**2. When this happened, I …** (Include your thoughts, speech, and actions.)

**3. The outcome of this was …**

**4. Based on what I learned in the video and On My Own exercises, I can prepare for future conflict by …** (Consider how your typical thoughts, speech, or actions might be changed in order to promote peace.)

To help with #4, you can look up the following verses.

- Proverbs 14:8
- Proverbs 12:18
- James 3:9–12

## CHART YOUR PROGRESS

Place a check in the boxes to identify how you are feeling in each area this week: emotionally, physically, etc. Even better? Substitute a word or two to describe how you are doing.

| | REALLY BAD | OKAY | PRETTY GOOD | GREAT |
|---|---|---|---|---|
| **Emotionally** | | | | |
| **Physically** | | | | |
| **Spiritually** (closeness to God) | | | | |
| **Relationally** (closeness to others) | | | | |
| **How your life is in general** | | | | |

# When your ex bad-mouths you in front of your child

Kids can feel overwhelming anxiety when parents fight and argue. Many times these fights happen when the children are nearby. Maybe you've been in a situation where your ex starts to criticize and belittle you—and your child is within earshot. What should you do?

You should remain calm. Sometimes the things we say or the attitude we have will make the situation worse. Later on, take these two steps:

## 1. Move toward your children

Once you're alone with your children, bring up what happened and gently ask what they thought about it. Be sure to listen without judgment, without offering your opinion, and without making them feel like they're taking sides.

### Ask and listen

- "When you heard Dad [Mom] say that about me, what did you think?"

- "Do you remember what you were doing when you heard our conversation?" (Many children think what they were doing at the time of the fight caused the divorce. Maybe your son was running a toy car against the wall when he heard the argument. For years he will think his running the car against the wall caused the divorce. Make sure they understand their actions didn't cause the divorce.)

### Affirm

"Thank you for sharing that with me. I'm glad we can share with each other."

Respond with grace (even though it's difficult, don't try to defend yourself): "I don't know why he [she] said that, but I know it's hard on you and I'm sorry."

### Reassure

- "I love you."

- "I care about you and how this affects you."

### Coach

- "Do you want to talk about what you could do or say the next time that happens?"

- The coaching part depends on the child's age and maturity. Discuss things the child might say when a dispute arises.

## 2. Move toward your former spouse

After your ex has cooled off, contact your ex and address this issue.

Ask your ex not to bad-mouth you in front of your children.

If you don't have open communication with your former spouse, this won't be possible. If it *is* possible, keep it simple and direct:

- "I've become aware that you said some things, and it's putting our kids in the middle."

- "I'd like to ask you not to say those kinds of things about me in front of our children, as it's putting them in an awkward situation."

Remember to stay calm and focused on your children.

When you talk with your former spouse about this issue, speak calmly and without a lot of emotion. The focus of the request should be on your children, not you. It's all about what this is doing to your kids, not how it makes you feel.

Your former spouse may respect the request to stop speaking badly about you in front of the children—or not. But at least you've done what you can do to promote peace, which Romans 12:18 tells us is all you can do in some situations: "If it is possible, as far as it depends on you, live at peace with everyone." By making that request, you've done your part to live that out. Then, continue to pray for your former spouse—for a change in heart and behavior—so you can truly live at peace with one another.

# DIVORCE*Care*

## *Living* FORWARD
### A GUIDED JOURNAL

## A guided journal for healing and direction

**Continue healing and prepare for your future**

Not sure about what lies ahead after your divorce or separation? This textured, hardcover journal can help you make sense of your emotions and make wise decisions for your future.

**Go deeper in your healing with the *Living Forward* journal.**

*"When I lay it all out on paper, I can see things clearer."*

Order your journal today: **divorcecare.org/journal**

# Forgiveness

*Learning how to let go, and why*

If your heart is raw from hurt, you might be tempted to skip this session altogether. But that will only prolong your pain and complicate your healing. Because the little-known truth about forgiveness is that it often benefits you more than it benefits the person who hurt you. So *you* need this.

Discover more often-overlooked reasons why that is true as you go through the **video**, **On My Own** exercises, and **My Weekly Journal** this week. You'll learn:

- **What forgiveness really is**
- **What forgiveness means for you**
- **What happens if you don't forgive**

Use this outline to write down important concepts, encouraging words, or questions you may have while viewing the video.

## THE TRAP OF BITTERNESS

It becomes your identity

It keeps you from moving on

## UNDERSTANDING FORGIVENESS

## FORGIVENESS IS NOT

Forgetting

Declaring your journey is over

> "Be kind to one another, tenderhearted, forgiving one another, as God in Christ forgave you."
>
> **Ephesians 4:32 ESV**

Excusing the person

> "For I will forgive
> their wickedness and will remember
> their sins no more."
>
> **Hebrews 8:12**

A feeling

## FORGIVENESS IS

A releasing of the person

> "If it is possible, as far as
> it depends on you,
> live at peace with everyone."
>
> **Romans 12:18**

A promise to the person

A gracious gift to the person

## FORGIVENESS CHALLENGES

Dealing with your unwillingness

Dealing with repeated offenses

Dealing with someone's negative reaction

## SEEKING FORGIVENESS

The 7 A's of confession

- Address everyone
- Avoid "if," "but," "maybe"
- Admit specific attitudes and actions
- Acknowledge the effects
- Accept the consequences
- Alter future behavior
- Ask, "Will you forgive me?"

## WALKING IN FORGIVENESS

### Additional help

# ON MY *Own*

## Wisdom and encouragement for your new journey

### VANEETHA'S STORY

*"I had to practice forgiveness on many levels: When I made plans and had to cancel them. When my ex hurt the girls and they were crying. When he called and accused me of something I hadn't done. I would get angry and roll things over in my head and think about all the things I was going to say. And that would just make me angrier. I realized that's poison."* This week, you'll learn what forgiveness is (and isn't) and how it can set you free from a burden you don't have to carry.

## 1 IS IT PAYBACK TIME?

It doesn't seem fair. Shouldn't that person have to pay? You want justice, and that's understandable. But this desire becomes an issue when you can't let go of your anger and hurt until the other person suffers too. Unforgiveness is a trap that lures you in with a taste for revenge, then leaves you stranded in bitterness, where you can never fully heal.

God wants a better future for you. He wants to walk with you through this, guiding you around that trap. This requires two things.

### 1. Release

"[Forgiveness] is not letting the person off the hook. It's putting the person on God's hook," explains Joy Forrest. God is just. He is all-knowing and far more capable than any human to carry out justice—so you can trust Him to do so.

Counselor Sabrina Black says, "Remember, God knows what happened and is going to deal with that situation. So you can rest and let God handle it." Tell God what you're thinking and feeling, and release it all into His capable hands. (Repeat this to yourself often!)

### 2. Refocus

Rather than spending precious energy on what you think should happen to the person, try shifting the focus to your own healing and to your relationship with God. Ask yourself: What steps can I take to forgive, heal, and grow? What can I do to draw closer to God in the midst of this?

You might:

- Pray and ask God to help you forgive

- Study what the Bible says about God's justice

- Speak with a mature Christian friend, pastor, or biblical counselor

- *[Add your own:]* _____

_____

*"Unforgiveness is like a wall between us and God."*
– Elsa Kok Colopy

## 2 BUT I'VE BEEN WRONGED!

When you've been hurt emotionally, it's easy to become bitter (replaying the incident in your mind, refusing to let it go, plotting what you'll do to get even). But did you know that this bitterness can wear you down emotionally, spiritually, *and* physically? That's why God has provided the cure for bitterness. It's forgiveness.

## GOD'S MESSAGE TO YOU

*"3 So watch yourselves. If your brother or sister sins against you, rebuke them; and if they repent, forgive them. 4 Even if they sin against you seven times in a day and seven times come back to you saying 'I repent,' you must forgive them."* (Luke 17:3–4)

1. **What personal hurts are you finding it hard to forgive right now? How has this been affecting you (physically, mentally, emotionally, spiritually)?**

2. **According to Luke 17:4, how often should you forgive someone? What do you think Jesus is trying to communicate here?**

## REMEMBER

- God knows that holding on to hurts from others will only hurt you more, so He wants you to forgive—again and again.

- Forgiveness is the heart of God's message for you. He expects you to forgive others because He provides forgiveness for you. See page103 to learn more about this gift.

*"Unforgiveness was eating me alive."* – Joy Forrest

## 3 HOW CAN I FORGIVE THAT PERSON?

When you've been hurt, there are really only two options. Your heart can grow bitter, or you can forgive.

## GOD'S MESSAGE TO YOU

*"31 Get rid of all bitterness, rage and anger, brawling and slander, along with every form of malice. 32 Be kind and compassionate to one another, forgiving each other, just as in Christ God forgave you."* (Ephesians 4:31–32)

1. **Do a quick heart check. Look at the traits that are listed in Ephesians 4:31 and 4:32. (They're very different!) Which best describes your current feelings and actions?**

2. According to these verses, how can you remove bitterness from your heart?




3. Based on today's verses, what should be your model and motivation for forgiving others?




## REMEMBER

- God's willingness to forgive all your faults and wrongs is a model of how you should treat others.

- When you forgive, you are driving bitterness from your life and replacing it with godly and healthy qualities.

*"Biblical forgiveness releases the right and craving to retaliate."* – Dr. Ramon Presson

 **4**

## WHAT FORGIVENESS LOOKS LIKE

*He went too far.*

*I couldn't possibly forgive her.*

Because forgiveness is *not* easy, you might not see how it's even possible in your situation. Read this parable (a story designed to teach a lesson) for a new perspective on forgiveness.

## GOD'S MESSAGE TO YOU

*"23 The kingdom of heaven is like a king who wanted to settle accounts with his servants. 24 As he began the settlement, a man who owed him ten thousand bags of gold was brought to him. 25 Since he was not able to pay, the master ordered that he and his wife and his children*

and all that he had be sold to repay the debt. *26 At this the servant fell on his knees before him. 'Be patient with me,' he begged, 'and I will pay back everything.' 27 The servant's master took pity on him, canceled the debt and let him go."* (Matthew 18:23–27)

1. **In Jesus' parable, the king represents God and the servant represents anyone who is in need of God's forgiveness. According to verse 27, how much did the king expect the man to pay back?**




2. **Based upon the king's decision, what lesson do you learn about God's willingness to forgive?**




3. **If you were the king, what impact would you want your act of forgiveness to have upon the servant?**




## REMEMBER

- To forgive means you no longer try to make the person "pay" for what was done to you. You cancel the debt, knowing that God will deal with your former spouse in a just and appropriate manner.

- Forgiveness doesn't mean you have to immediately trust the person who hurt you. It only makes trusting possible.

*"If God did this for me, I can extend this gift to others."* – Keith Battle

## 5 WHY SHOULD I FORGIVE THAT PERSON?

You might be surprised to hear what happens next in the story about the servant and the king (see day 4). After the king forgave the man's debt, here's what the servant did ...

### GOD'S MESSAGE TO YOU

"*28 But when that servant went out, he found one of his fellow servants who owed him a hundred silver coins. He grabbed him and began to choke him. 'Pay back what you owe me!' he demanded. 29 His fellow servant fell to his knees and begged him, 'Be patient with me, and I will pay it back.' 30 But he refused. ...*

"*32 Then the master called the servant in. ... He said, 'I canceled all that debt of yours because you begged me to. 33 Shouldn't you have had mercy on your fellow servant just as I had on you?'*" (Matthew 18:28–30a, 32–33)

1. **When you read how the servant responded to his fellow servant—after having been fully forgiven himself—what parallels do you see with people who want their ex-spouse to "pay them back"?**

2. **Think about how God has forgiven you. How does this compare to the way you've forgiven others?**

### REMEMBER

- "If we see ourselves as all good, we won't be as apt to offer forgiveness. We need to see ourselves in our true state, desperately in need [of forgiveness], and then in turn, understand and have compassion on other people who need it too." – Georgia Shaffer

- When you appreciate how much God has forgiven you, you can be willing to forgive others.

## VANEETHA'S STORY

"*Forgiveness has been a big part of my journey, and it begins with the decision to forgive. But it's not a one-time thing. It's a process you go through over and over again. Literally every day I begged God, 'Don't let me be bitter. Don't let me keep holding on to this.' And [forgiving my ex-husband] has been the most life-giving, life-changing thing I have ever done.*

"*I think the hardest part is that we think we're letting somebody off the hook. Nothing could be further from the truth. We're actually saying there's nothing you can do to make up for it. So, I just have to forgive you—like Christ died for me and forgave me.*"

### NEXT SESSION

Pursuing a civil relationship with your ex.

# MY WEEKLY Journal

If you struggle with bitterness, use your weekly journal to write about your experience. You can use these prompts:

1. I am struggling to forgive …

2. I am having trouble letting go of …

3. Because I'm holding on to this, I've felt … and done …

4. When it comes to forgiveness, the video and On My Own exercises have taught me …

As you journal about forgiveness, it will be helpful to read and think about:

- Psalm 103:12
- Micah 7:18–19
- Colossians 3:13

## CHART YOUR PROGRESS

Place a check in the boxes to identify how you are feeling in each area this week: emotionally, physically, etc. Even better? Substitute a word or two to describe how you are doing.

| | REALLY BAD | OKAY | PRETTY GOOD | GREAT |
|---|---|---|---|---|
| Emotionally | | | | |
| Physically | | | | |
| Spiritually (closeness to God) | | | | |
| Relationally (closeness to others) | | | | |
| How your life is in general | | | | |

# FOR *Parents*

## *Helping your kids understand (and practice!) forgiveness*

Helping your children learn about forgiveness can be the most precious gift you give them. Here are simple ways to teach your children what forgiveness is and to help them develop a forgiving heart.

### Explain what forgiveness is

Start by giving them an age-appropriate explanation of forgiveness. You can break it down this way:

**Unforgiveness says**

1. But it was her fault!

2. I want to hurt him back!

3. I'm gonna stay mad at that person forever!

**Forgiveness says**

1. I won't expect the person to pay me back for what he or she has done.

2. I trust that God will deal with the person.

3. I'm going to move on without holding a grudge.

### Provide examples of forgiveness

To help your children understand what forgiveness looks like, share examples. You could:

- Share stories from your own life about forgiveness.

- Allow other adults to give examples of how they've forgiven someone.

- Role-play forgiving others. Start with simple scenarios, such as "Someone hits you at school because you're in his way. What kind, forgiving things could you say?"

- Tell Bible stories about forgiveness. Jesus is the greatest example.

You can also provide examples from the child's life. For instance, "When your sister was little and used to take your toys when you said not to, you forgave her."

### Teach them how to ask for forgiveness

This will take practice. Encourage them to practice by saying, "I'm sorry. Will you forgive me?" in front of the bathroom mirror. Then gently remind them to say this when dealing with their siblings, you, their friends, and anyone else they hurt in small and big ways.

### Teach them why they should forgive

Children love to ask, "Why?" When they ask, "Why should I forgive?" say, "We forgive because God forgave us. And when we don't forgive, our unforgiveness separates us from God and separates us from other people."

To explain these points, share the story of the unforgiving servant found in Matthew 18:21–35.

You can also share this forgiveness illustration: Ask your children to pick up a large trash can (or you pick it up). The trash inside the can represents all the bad things people have done to them that they have not forgiven. They have to carry it around with them 24/7. How easy is it to do anything with other people with a giant trash can in their arms? When you forgive, you throw the trash away, and you can live freely and have relationships again.

# RECEIVING *Forgiveness*

Vaneetha, Richard, and Craig each found themselves in a maze of bitterness, unable to escape. In this week's video, you learned how they were able to exit the maze—by forgiving their former spouses. But what enabled them to do that? Didn't they have a right to be bitter?

Not when they considered how much God forgave them. As Chuck said, "If I can be forgiven, why can't I [too] forgive my ex-wife?"

## WHAT DO YOU NEED FORGIVENESS FOR?

Even if you don't find yourself in a maze of bitterness, you might be trapped in some other wrong behavior patterns, such as anger, self-pity, a desire for revenge, spitefulness, addiction, or doing anything to escape the pain. As a matter of fact, we all find ourselves making wrong choices in life, as we respond to people and circumstances around us. And that's why we need God's forgiveness.

God calls our wrong choices "sin" because they fall short of the standards He set for us. Our failures also offend God because they represent a willful rejection of God Himself, His nature, and His ways. Our choice to sin is an approval of what He stands against.

Because sin is the rejection of God and what is right, God, being just, must punish it. (Otherwise He'd be guilty of approving of evil.) As Romans 6:23 explains, "For the wages [what we deserve] of sin is death." Thankfully, that verse goes on to explain, "But the gift of God is eternal life in Christ Jesus our Lord."

## GOD OFFERS YOU FREE AND UNDESERVED FORGIVENESS

God made the gift of forgiveness available through Jesus, His Son. Jesus lived a perfect life (for you!). Then He gave His life for you—paying the price for your sin, making it possible for you to be forgiven and stand before God without fear of judgment.

John 3:16 says, "For God so loved the world that he gave his one and only Son, that whoever believes in him shall not perish but have eternal life."

## SEE HOW MUCH GOD FORGIVES YOU

God offers forgiveness for every wrong we've ever done and ever will do. When you accept God's forgiveness, you are then in a place to offer forgiveness to others. Because, ultimately, God wants our forgiveness to reflect His own. In order to do that, you need to first receive forgiveness from Him.

Because of Jesus' death on the cross for you, you can ask God to forgive your wrong choices, your sins. Would you like to ask God to forgive you? If so, you can use this prayer. Say to God:

*God, I know I'm a sinner ... For too long, I've ignored or rejected You ... Thank you for allowing Jesus to suffer and die in my place ... Please forgive me for my sins ... Help me live the life You desire for me ... In Jesus' name. Amen.*

If you've prayed this prayer, you are starting a new life following Jesus.

## I PRAYED THE PRAYER ASKING GOD FOR FORGIVENESS. WHAT'S NEXT?

The Bible says, if anyone is in Christ, he is a new creation. The old is GONE. The NEW has come (2 Corinthians 5:17). Now that you've been forgiven, you will better understand how you can, in turn, forgive others (with God's help). You have started on a new path, walking with Jesus. And He will continue to guide you and transform your life as you let Him lead you.

Your next steps are to devote time to studying God's Word, to prayer, and to spending time with others who will encourage you on your journey of following Christ. Let your DivorceCare leaders know you have asked God for forgiveness, so they can help guide you in your next steps.

# YOUR *Former* SPOUSE

## *Figuring out what's next*

What now? You're no longer together, but your lives are still connected. So, what kind of relationship should you have with your former spouse?

This week's **video**, **On My Own** exercises, and **My Weekly Journal** will help you explore the possibilities and decide where to go from here. You'll discover:

- **What a civil relationship with your ex-spouse might look like**
- **When a new type of friendship with your former spouse might be possible**
- **What to consider before thinking about remarrying your ex**

Use this outline to write down important concepts, encouraging words, or questions you may have while viewing the video.

## THE THREE PATHS

Ensure your emotional and physical safety

Responding to an abusive ex-spouse

- Contact the courthouse about an order of protection
- Contact your bank about the status of joint accounts
- Contact a family law attorney about options to protect your children

## CAMP CIVILITY

Don't join the argument culture

> *"If it be possible,*
> *as much as lieth in you,*
> *live peaceably with all men."*
>
> **Romans 12:18 KJV**

Commit to a forgiving attitude

## CHOOSING A PATH

Co-parenting

Friendship

Remarriage

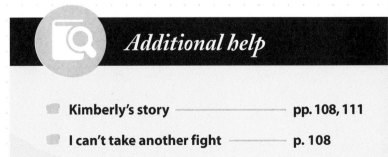

### Additional help

| | |
|---|---|
| 📖 **Kimberly's story** ———————— | **pp. 108, 111** |
| 📖 **I can't take another fight** ———— | **p. 108** |
| 📖 **Has my former spouse changed?** — | **p. 111** |

# ON MY *Own*

## *Wisdom and encouragement for your new journey*

### KIMBERLY'S STORY

*"For a long time, my ex-husband was an enemy to me, and that was not a good place to be. We became triggers for each other. And you can't avoid that trigger when you have kids and you're trying to co-parent! He would text a jab at me, and I would send one right back. We were just tearing each other down."* This week, you'll learn how Kimberly got to a better place with her ex and what steps she took (and you can take) to get there.

### 1 I CAN'T TAKE ANOTHER FIGHT

World peace would be nice—but right now you'd settle for peace in your own household. If the conflicts seem unending, you're probably ready for some relief. You can find it in today's verses.

## GOD'S MESSAGE TO YOU

*"**22** But the Holy Spirit produces this kind of fruit in our lives: love, joy, peace, patience, kindness, goodness, faithfulness, **23** gentleness, and self-control. There is no law against these things!"* (Galatians 5:22–23 NLT)

1. **Today's verses list the fruit (something produced) that comes as a result of God's Spirit working in a person's life. Underline one or two that you could really use more of in your life.**

2. **If you cultivated this fruit in your life (encouraged it to grow), how would that reduce the amount of conflict you have?**

3. **Write out one example of conflict from the past month that would have gone better if that fruit had been growing.**

## REMEMBER

- If you follow God, His Spirit will produce fruit (godly traits) in you.

- Some conflict between humans is inevitable, but the fruit of the Holy Spirit can reduce the amount of conflict in your life.

## 2 | I WAS WRONGED. WHY SHOULD I INITIATE?

God took the initiative to love us when we were un-lovable and we didn't love Him. And He calls us to love others as He has loved us. With God's help, there are practical steps you can take to initiate reconciliation. For you, reconciliation might mean civility; it might mean friendship; it might mean something more (including the possibility of restoring your marriage). The goal is a peaceful restoration, as much as is possible from your end.

## GOD'S MESSAGE TO YOU

*"But God demonstrates his own love for us in this: While we were still sinners, Christ died for us."* (Romans 5:8)

*"He saved us, not because of righteous things we had done, but because of his mercy."* (Titus 3:5a)

*"This is love: not that we loved God, but that he loved us and sent his Son as an atoning sacrifice for our sins."* (1 John 4:10)

1. **According to Romans 5 and Titus 3, how much did we deserve God's love, especially His saving us from our sins?**

2. **Think about your relationship with your former spouse. Even if restoring the marriage isn't possible, how can you still show love and kindness?**

3. **Why do you think God calls us to initiate the restoration of relationships, even when the other person isn't necessarily willing?**

## REMEMBER

- Restoring broken relationships is important to God. It should be important to you too.

- "If it is possible, as far as it depends on you, live at peace with everyone." (Romans 12:18)

- Full restoration of your marriage is a wonderful thing, but for some people it's not possible or wise.

## 3 | WHAT DO I DO WHEN MY EX IS HARD TO LOVE?

Some people are easier to love than others. But with everything that's happened, there might be certain people you think are impossible to love. And on your own, that might be true. But God has a different perspective.

## GOD'S MESSAGE TO YOU

*"**43** You have heard that it was said, 'Love your neighbor and hate your enemy.' **44** But I tell you, love your enemies and pray for those who persecute you, **45** that you may be children of your Father in heaven. ... **46** If you love those who love you, what reward will you get? Are not even the tax collectors [the corrupt and greedy] doing that? **47** And if you greet only your own people, what are you doing more than others?"* (Matthew 5:43–47a)

1. **Is there anyone in your life you would consider your enemy? Anyone who persecutes (harasses) you? What do today's verses say you should do to these people?**

**2. Why is it easier to love some people than others? What do today's verses say about loving only those who are loving toward you?**

**3. What is one thing you could do this week to start applying today's verses to your life? Choose one of the following:**

☐ Pray for your former spouse

☐ Offer to help with the kids (or something else) outside of your normal obligations

☐ Other _____

## REMEMBER

- Godly love extends to those who are hard to love—even your enemies.

- When you love your enemies, you are imitating God and living as His child.

*"I can grow and do what God wants me to do."*
– Richard

## 4 I'M SORRY—BUT NOT REALLY

If you catch a kid using his cell phone after you told him not to, he might regret disobeying. But is he sorry that he disobeyed or that he got caught? A good way to tell is whether he apologizes sincerely and obeys you the next time—or does it again.

Paul, the writer of 2 Corinthians, talks about a similar situation between people and God.

## GOD'S MESSAGE TO YOU

*"For the kind of sorrow God wants us to experience leads us away from sin and results in salvation [God's rescue, keeping you safe eternally]. There's no regret for that kind of sorrow. But worldly sorrow, which lacks repentance, results in spiritual death."* (2 Corinthians 7:10 NLT)

*"Prove by the way you live that you have repented of your sins and turned to God."* (Luke 3:8a NLT)

**1. Think about a time you said "I'm sorry" to your former spouse for something you did. What was your underlying motivation?**

**2. According to 2 Corinthians 7:10, what happens when someone experiences "worldly sorrow" (being concerned about themselves, and not about pleasing God) over their behavior? What happens if they experience godly sorrow?**

**3. Repentance is changing your thinking about a behavior, which leads to changing the behavior to please God. What does Luke 3:8 say is the evidence of repentance?**

## REMEMBER

- It's possible to be "sorry" about something without truly repenting.

- Godly sorrow, which leads to repentance, is important for moving forward in your recovery—and it's essential if you want to reconcile with your spouse.

*"I've got to go on being the best me that I can be."*
– Doug

## 5 HAS MY FORMER SPOUSE REALLY CHANGED?

Maybe your former spouse made wrong choices that instigated the breakup (e.g., an affair or abuse), but now wants to get back together. Before you can consider restoring the marriage, your ex needs to do more than say "I'm sorry; I'll never do it again." God calls him or her to repent. Repentance involves:

1. Recognizing and admitting the wrong.

2. Choosing to completely turn away from that wrong behavior.

3. Intentionally and consistently choosing God-pleasing behavior.

True repentance should occur before remarriage.

## GOD'S MESSAGE TO YOU

*"Produce fruit in keeping with repentance."* (Matthew 3:8)

*"22 But the Holy Spirit produces this kind of fruit in our lives: love, joy, peace, patience, kindness, goodness, faithfulness, 23 gentleness, and self-control."* (Galatians 5:22–23a NLT)

**1. What changes has your former spouse made in his or her life since the divorce?**

**2. Look at the type of fruit that God expects in our lives (Galatians 5:22–23a). Which specific changes can you look for in your former spouse if there has been repentance?**

3. If you are the spouse who caused the divorce for non-biblical reasons (perhaps because of an affair or other sinful behavior), what is your role in reconciliation?

## REMEMBER

- Reconciliation requires both spouses to repent for the wrongs done in a marriage.

- "They should repent and turn to God and demonstrate their repentance by their deeds." (Acts 26:20b)

## KIMBERLY'S STORY

*"Being saturated with God's Word and having the DivorceCare homework to go over during the week gave me the foundation to rediscover myself and stop hating him. That hate was what was holding me back from enjoying life in abundance.*

*"Until I forgave him, I didn't have the capacity to pray for him or to fully invite him back into his child's life. I couldn't do that through my anger. So Christ's love was crucial in getting me on the path to being open to the new dynamic of co-parenting. Last Christmas, we talked about making sure he sees our son more often. And I realized we both have grown, because the conversation never went anywhere negative."*

## NEXT SESSION

How to adjust to being single again.

# MY WEEKLY Journal

Are interactions with your former spouse stressful? Confusing? Journaling can help you sort through the emotions as you find a way to move forward. Use the following prompts to organize your thoughts.

1. When I think about my former spouse, I feel …

2. In response to those thoughts and feelings, when I'm with my former spouse, I tend to …

3. Our interactions could be less stressful and healthier if I …

4. Two things I learned from the video and On My Own exercises that can help me with these interactions are …

## CHART YOUR PROGRESS

Place a check in the boxes to identify how you are feeling in each area this week: emotionally, physically, etc. Even better? Substitute a word or two to describe how you are doing.

|  | REALLY BAD | OKAY | PRETTY GOOD | GREAT |
|---|---|---|---|---|
| Emotionally |  |  |  |  |
| Physically |  |  |  |  |
| Spiritually (closeness to God) |  |  |  |  |
| Relationally (closeness to others) |  |  |  |  |
| How your life is in general |  |  |  |  |

# FOR *Parents*

## *My kids don't want to see my ex*

Your children aren't excited about visiting your former spouse. They might not even want to see your ex at all. What are you supposed to do, especially when the court has granted certain visitation rights?

To help children who find themselves in this difficult situation, try these two steps.

### 1. Find out what's going on with your children

The struggle your children are having is a common one. But the reasons vary. Talk to them to find out why they want to avoid the other parent. Here are some reasons children often give:

- *"I don't want my mom [dad] to feel bad if they know I'm having fun with my other parent."* (Your children don't want to betray you, so they'll try to make you feel better by saying they don't want to go.)

- *"I'm worried about what will happen at home while I'm gone."* (They're concerned their stepbrother will go in their room, or they'll miss out on fun activities.)

- *"It's lonely at my dad's."* (The other parent doesn't have time or doesn't make an effort to see them while they are there.)

- *"My mom is so sad that it's hard to be around her."* (The other parent is depressed or angry, so time with that parent is not enjoyable.)

- *"It's scary over there."* (It's an unfamiliar environment, or the child might truly receive poor treatment.)

If you can determine why your children don't want to see your former spouse, you can take steps to help them handle the situation better. For example, you could calm any fears about what might happen while they're gone, or offer suggestions for how to avoid loneliness while they're at the other home.

Note: If you suspect your children have legitimate safety reasons for wanting to avoid your former spouse, it's important to take appropriate steps, as outlined on page 79.

### 2. Help your children cope

Often, a few simple steps can make a big impact on how your children handle this situation.

- **Offer empathy:** Feel for your children and what they are experiencing. Listen to their concerns. Even if you can't change the situation, knowing they are heard and understood can help.

- **Provide comfort:** Give your children items that can bring comfort. For small children, this might mean allowing them to bring a familiar blanket or stuffed animal with them when they visit the other parent. For older children, perhaps a journal or sketch pad would give them an outlet to turn to while at the other home.

- **Avoid alienating:** Be careful how you speak about the other parent while your children are around. Bashing your ex-spouse or purposely trying to alienate your children from your ex will only make things harder for the kids.

- **Give Scriptures:** Share Bible verses that will resonate with your children. Examples include "You are my hiding place; you will protect me from trouble" (Psalm 32:7a) and "Be strong and courageous … for the LORD your God goes with you; he will never leave you nor forsake you" (Deuteronomy 31:6). Encourage them to memorize these verses, or give them something with these verses written on them as a reminder of these important truths.

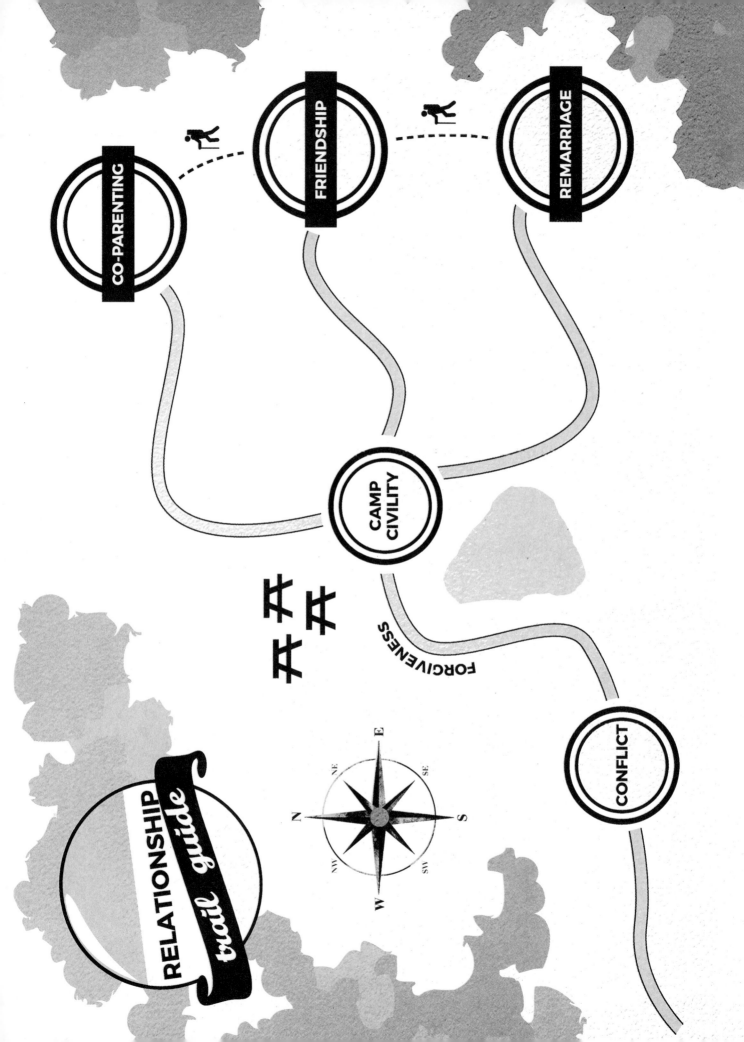

# Single LIVING

## *Rethinking your identity*

*This is not where I expected to be at this point in my life. What now? Start dating? Stay single?*

Everyone's story is different. So what should the next chapter of your life look like?

Use this week's **video**, **On My Own** exercises, and **My Weekly Journal** to help you decide what's next for you as you explore single living. Discover:

- **How to rethink your life as an unmarried person**
- **How to trust others again**
- **What it means to be content**
- **The purpose and pitfalls of dating**

## VIDEO OUTLINE

Use this outline to write down important concepts, encouraging words, or questions you may have while viewing the video.

## PREPARE FOR A NEW ROLE

Let God define who you are

- Choose God's truth over your feelings

> "I praise you because I am fearfully and wonderfully made; your works are wonderful, I know that full well."
>
> **Psalm 139:14**

Be willing to try new things

> "All this stuff that's happened to me ... I can either let it be my identity, or I can let it be part of my story."
>
> **Chuck**

## LEARN TO TRUST OTHERS

Trusting God is the foundation

Trusting others is a process

## DATING

Are you comfortable with your "new normal"?

Are you looking for a godly partner—or a warm body?

Are you looking for opportunities for mutual growth?

> "'For this reason a man will leave his father and mother and be united to his wife, and the two will become one flesh'? So they are no longer two, but one flesh."
>
> **Matthew 19:5–6a**

# DIVORCE IN THE BIBLE

It's permitted in cases of adultery

> "But if the unbeliever leaves, let it be so. The brother or the sister is not bound in such circumstances."
>
> **1 Corinthians 7:15a**

It's permitted in cases of abandonment

# REMARRIAGE

How did your divorce align with God's plan for marriage and divorce?

What have you learned about your contribution to the breakup of the marriage?

Does the other person have a genuine and personal relationship with Jesus?

Does the other person view the covenant of marriage like I do?

## Additional help

How are you doing? ——————— p. 118

If I only had _____ , I'd be happy —— p. 120

Sex outside of marriage? ——————— p. 121

# ON MY *Own*

## *Wisdom and encouragement for your new journey*

### TIFFANY'S STORY

*"How did I know I was ready for dating? When I met my current husband, we dated a long time before talking about marriage. I wanted to make sure he treated my daughters well and that they accepted him. I needed to make sure he had a strong relationship with Christ and would be a good role model for my children. I watched how he treated his own family—and I saw this during all four seasons, multiple times."* Whether you're considering dating, remaining single, or seeking reconciliation with your former spouse, this week will help you decide your next steps.

## 1 HOW ARE YOU DOING?

How about a quick pause to evaluate how your life is going right now? Here's a simple tool from Sabrina Black to help you get a clear snapshot. It's called the Wheel of Life.

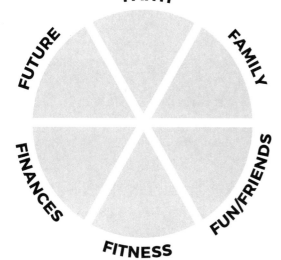

The wheel is divided into 6 major areas that affect your life health. Rank each area with a number from 0 to 10. Ten means you're doing great in that area. Zero means you need a whole lot of help. To determine your numbers, ask yourself questions. (For faith: Am I spending time reading my Bible? For family: Am I spending quality time with my kids?)

The goal is to help you see what areas might need some work. For example, if your finances are a 9, but your family is a 2, you probably need to shift some focus to your family. Once you finish, it can be helpful to ask someone how he or she would score you in each category, then compare that to the rankings you gave yourself. This input can reveal weaknesses and strengths you might not see.

Decide which areas need improvement, then take small steps forward to raise your number. Be patient. If you think you're a 3 in one area, don't expect to be a 10 overnight. Work on moving it toward a 5 or 6 for now, to create more balance in your life.

## 2    A NEW PERSPECTIVE

Would running 10 miles as punishment feel different from running 10 miles to train for a race you might win? Changing your perspective doesn't change the difficulty of the work, but it does affect your attitude and responses.

Today's verses will help you to see your difficulties from a new perspective and give you confidence that there is life on the other side of divorce.

## GOD'S MESSAGE TO YOU

*"6 So be truly glad. There is wonderful joy ahead, even though you must endure many trials for a little while. 7 These trials will show that your faith is genuine. It is being tested as fire tests and purifies gold—though your faith is far more precious than mere gold. So when your faith remains strong through many trials, it will bring you much praise and glory and honor on the day when Jesus Christ is revealed to the whole world."* (1 Peter 1:6–7 NLT)

*"3 We can rejoice, too, when we run into problems and trials, for we know that they help us develop endurance. 4 And endurance develops strength of character, and character strengthens our confident hope of salvation."* (Romans 5:3–4 NLT)

1. **What trials are you facing? How does 1 Peter 1:6–7 say you could look at these hardships?**

2. **What can your struggles produce, according to today's verses?**

3. **When gold is purified by fire, the refiner continues to reheat it and remove impurities until he can see his reflection in the gold— then he knows it's ready. How have you seen this happening in your own life?**

## REMEMBER

- "Our circumstances change all the time. Ultimately, my joy comes out of knowing [God] and the fact that His purpose for my life will be completed." – Dr. Crawford Loritts

- Pain has a purpose—and the end result is glorious.

- Your suffering is temporary, but hope in what Christ has done is eternal.

## 3    HOW GOD MEETS YOUR NEEDS

God meets our needs by giving us Himself (His presence) and by placing us in a community with other people.

## GOD'S MESSAGE TO YOU

**God's presence:**

*"You will fill me with joy in your [God's] presence, with eternal pleasures at your right hand."* (Psalm 16:11b)

*"When you go through deep waters, I will be with you. When you go through rivers of difficulty, you will not drown. When you walk through the fire of oppression, you will not be burned up; the flames will not consume you."* (Isaiah 43:2 NLT)

**Community of other believers:**

*"17 I pray that you, being rooted and established in love, 18 may have power, together with all the Lord's holy people, to grasp how wide and long and high and deep is the love of Christ, 19 and to know this love that*

*surpasses knowledge—that you may be filled to the measure of all the fullness of God."* (Ephesians 3:17b–19)

1. **Describe the benefits of God's presence in your life (see today's verses).**

2. **Being in community (relationship) with others who believe in Jesus is one way we grow in our understanding of how much God loves us. How does Ephesians 3 describe God's love?**

3. **How has your understanding of God's love grown as you've participated in your DivorceCare group?**

## REMEMBER

- "God created us so that we would need each other. One of the gifts He gives to us is the supportive community and fellowship within the church." – Dr. Ramon Presson

- Asking for and accepting help is an important part of living in a community and being in relationship with others.

**4** **IF I ONLY HAD _____, I'D BE HAPPY** _____

Your life looks different than it used to. There might be things you wish you had, but you don't. Are you able to be content with what you do have? This isn't always easy—but there's a secret to contentment you can find in today's verses.

## GOD'S MESSAGE TO YOU

*"**11** I have learned how to be content with whatever I have. **12** I know how to live on almost nothing or with everything. I have learned the secret of living in every situation, whether it is with a full stomach or empty, with plenty or little. **13** For I can do everything through Christ, who gives me strength."* (Philippians 4:11b–13 NLT)

1. **Paul wrote these words when he was in prison. Earlier in his life, he had been influential and wealthy. Describe a time when you remember having enough and a time when you remember wanting more of something.**

2. **What is your attitude when you have enough of what you want? What about when you don't have what you want?**

3. **Contentment means being satisfied with what God has provided, at whatever level He has decided to provide. But it's hard to be content. According to today's verses, how could you be content with whatever you have?** (Hint: Reread the last sentence of the verses.)

## REMEMBER

- Joy and contentment aren't ultimately based on circumstances—they are dependent on your relationship with Jesus.

- God has given you enough to be content. And we can be satisfied with that, and thankful.

*"Your identity is not in your marital state."*
– Dr. Stephen Viars

## 5 WHY NOT HAVE SEX OUTSIDE OF MARRIAGE?

God created sex. And understanding His purposes for sex is key to enjoying it fully and wisely. Here are some of the reasons why God created sex:

- To allow husbands and wives to give and receive pleasure – Proverbs 5:18–19

- To create a unique, unbreakable union – Genesis 2:24

- To present a picture of the union between Christ and the church – Ephesians 5:32

## THE PROBLEM WITH SEX OUTSIDE OF MARRIAGE

While pleasurable, sex outside of God's design brings negative consequences. To start, there's the chance of unwanted pregnancy and sexually transmitted disease. Sex outside of marriage often leads to painful emotional fallout, such as heartbreak, uncertainty, doubt, depression, and fear. It's also self-centered. Even if you're okay with it, you never know the impact it will have on the other person. Plus, you are enticing someone else to disobey God, and sex outside of marriage doesn't reflect the bond God wants it to represent.

## GOD IS SERIOUS ABOUT THIS

When we understand the purpose of sex and the potential consequences of its misuse, it's easier to understand why God is serious about it being enjoyed the way He designed it to be.

*"Let there be no sexual immorality [sex outside of marriage], impurity, or greed among you. Such sins have no place among God's people. … Don't be fooled by those who try to excuse these sins, for the anger of God will fall on all who disobey him."* (Ephesians 5:3, 6 NLT)

## PUTTING IT INTO PRACTICE

What steps of accountability can you put in place to protect yourself from sexual immorality?

*"We dated for seven years. We remained pure."* – Mike

**BRIGHTER DAYS**

## TIFFANY'S STORY

*"Throughout our long courtship, my future husband always put my needs and my kids' needs before his. Our relationship was a true reflection of what God created oneness to look like. I saw how he cherished his family, and we always went to church together and did devotions together. Over time, this man proved to me that he was solid, so when he proposed, I accepted."*

## NEXT SESSION

Brighter days are ahead for you.

# MY WEEKLY
## *Journal*

As you consider what single living might look like for you, use your journal to sort through the possibilities.

**1. My biggest concern about being single is …**

**2. I find myself thinking/dreaming/worrying most about …**

**3. This causes me to …**

As you think about your responses and actions for prompt #3, it will be helpful to look up the following verses and think about the powerful truths found there.

- Romans 8:37–39

- Ephesians 5:1–2

- 1 John 3:1

## CHART YOUR PROGRESS

Place a check in the boxes to identify how you are feeling in each area this week: emotionally, physically, etc. Even better? Substitute a word or two to describe how you are doing.

| | REALLY BAD | OKAY | PRETTY GOOD | GREAT |
|---|---|---|---|---|
| **Emotionally** | | | | |
| **Physically** | | | | |
| **Spiritually** (closeness to God) | | | | |
| **Relationally** (closeness to others) | | | | |
| **How your life is in general** | | | | |

# FOR Parents

## Lightening the load: Single-parent help

Parenting solo is a big job. Some days you probably wish you had a maid, a chauffeur, a nanny, and 36 hours instead of 24.

We can't do anything about the 24-hour limit to the day, but we can point you to some great stress-relieving ideas. Single parents are finding the following tools valuable for managing time and helping kids adjust to a single-parent household. They've discovered it's possible not only to maintain your sanity as a single parent, but to thrive in the role!

### Free, stress-relieving resource: Nature!

Do you have a child with unruly behavior? Kids who are trying to adjust to the divorce or separation can be stressed, scared, and angry, and have a barrage of other emotions. Guess what can help soothe that stress and calm them down? Nature.

Going outside puts kids in contact with God's beautiful creation. And it helps both parents and kids to be more relaxed, sleep better, laugh more, enjoy better moods, and find it easier to come together as a family. Share with your kids the truths written long ago in Psalm 19: "The heavens declare the glory of God; the skies proclaim the work of his hands. Day after day they pour forth speech; night after night they reveal knowledge."

So, the occasional video game or movie is okay, but be sure to encourage outdoor activities, even if it's just sitting and gazing at the clouds.

### Divvying up the household tasks

Here's a relief: You don't need to be the only one responsible for maintaining your home. When you teach your children to contribute, they not only learn life skills they'll need as an adult, but they also feel more connected to the family. Yes, they may complain at first, but it will be better for everyone in the long run as they contribute and connect. Make it a point to have fun with the family chores. Perhaps have a race to see who finishes first.

A family meeting, where you discuss the things that need to be done on a daily or weekly basis, is good. Then, divide and conquer. Give everyone responsibilities—and don't underestimate young children. There are six-year-olds who do their own laundry (and are better at operating modern, high-tech machines than their parents!). Even if your children visit rarely, it is still important for them to contribute to the home environment.

Give your children some freedom in choosing which responsibilities they want to make their own. Maybe one enjoys raking the yard, while another doesn't mind doing dishes.

### Single & Parenting videos

Single & Parenting is a free online resource for single parents. You'll have access to weekly videos on crucial single-parenting topics and a downloadable book similar to your DivorceCare participant guide. Visit **divorcecare.org/my** and take advantage of the tips, encouragement, and teaching that will help you manage your single-parenting challenges.

### Additional resources from DivorceCare

Visit **DivorceCare's ParentZone, dc4k.org/parentzone**, for great resources from others who have been where you are. Helpful videos, uplifting messages, and inspiring articles are available to review, for free.

# DIVORCE & *Remarriage*

### *A decision-making tool kit*

There are two circumstances in which God explicitly permits divorce. If your spouse was sexually unfaithful or if you are a Christian and your nonbelieving spouse abandoned you, the Bible says you are free to divorce and to marry someone else. But you might be wondering, "The circumstances surrounding my divorce were different from those mentioned in the Bible, so can I remarry?" Or maybe you're wondering whether to remarry your former spouse. If you have these questions, we want to introduce you to our decision-making tool kit. These tools are ways in which God's Spirit guides His people.

## PRAYER

As you seek to make a wise decision, start by praying. Prayer is simply telling God what's on your heart. James 1:5–6a says, "If any of you lacks wisdom, you should ask God, who gives generously to all without finding fault, and it will be given to you. But when you ask, you must believe and not doubt."

## BIBLE STUDY

The Bible is God's Word to us. It "thoroughly equips" us to live lives pleasing to God (2 Timothy 3:17). Even if it doesn't directly answer your specific questions, the more familiar you are with its instructions, examples, and principles, the better able you'll be to evaluate different possible answers to those questions.

## WISE COUNSEL

Proverbs 15:22 says, "Plans fail for lack of counsel, but with many advisers they succeed." If you're confused about your circumstances and whether or not you should get a divorce and are free to remarry—or if you have other questions not clearly addressed in Scripture—find a pastor or another mature Christian who can help you understand what biblical principles might apply to your situation.

## CHURCH DISCIPLINE AND RESTORATION PROCESS

This tool can be used when you've been wronged by your spouse (or your ex-spouse) and are trying to decide whether to restore or end the marriage. It is a formal procedure your church can use to help guide your decision, which is described in Matthew 18:15–17a: "If your brother or sister sins, go and point out their fault, just between the two of you. ... If they will not listen, take one or two others along, so that 'every matter may be established by the testimony of two or three witnesses.' If they still refuse to listen, tell it to the church." Talk with your pastor to see if this process fits your situation. This is God's way to resolve conflicts, and marriages have been joyfully restored through this process. But even if your marriage is not restored, your church leaders will be in a better position to advise you about your divorce.

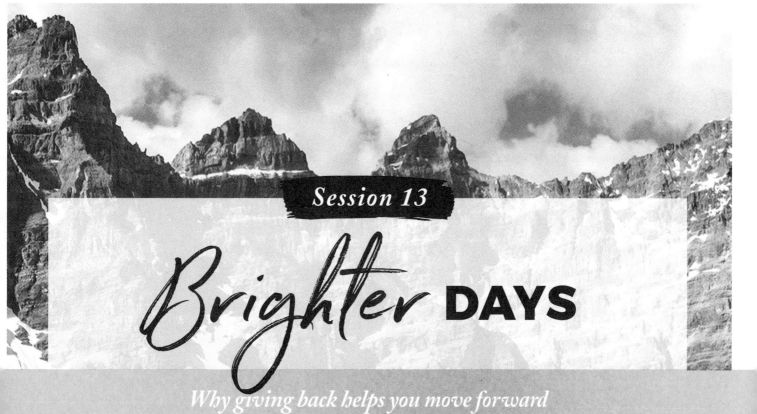

# Brighter DAYS

*Why giving back helps you move forward*

You've learned so much over the past few weeks. Now, find out how to use what you've learned to brighten not only *your* future, but the lives of others too.

In this week's **video**, **On My Own** exercises, and **My Weekly Journal**, you'll discover:

- **How others are using the lessons God taught them through divorce**
- **Ways to find hope when more difficulties inevitably arise**
- **How serving others contributes to your recovery**

# VIDEO OUTLINE

Use this outline to write down important concepts, encouraging words, or questions you may have while viewing the video.

## LEARNING CONTENTMENT

Contentment is based on your choices

- Choose truth
- Choose joy (focus on the blessings you have in Christ)
- Choose faith
- Choose community
- Choose service

> *"Whatsoever things are true, whatsoever things are honest, whatsoever things are just, whatsoever things are pure, whatsoever things are lovely, whatsoever things are of good report ... think on these things."*
>
> **Philippians 4:8 KJV**

## REACHING OUT TO OTHERS

> *"Praise be to the God and Father of our Lord Jesus Christ, the Father of compassion and the God of all comfort, who comforts us in all our troubles, so that we can comfort those in any trouble with the comfort we ourselves receive from God."*
>
> **2 Corinthians 1:3–4**

# LOSS & A NEW DIRECTION

127

# ON MY *Own*

## *Wisdom and encouragement for your new journey*

### MARY LOU'S STORY

*"There's a time to mourn, to experience the sadness, the loneliness, the loss, and the tears that come with that. But then on the other side of that, I want to move forward. Yes, this has been a terrible thing, but what can happen now? It's a clean slate that I think something new can be written on. And it's exciting."* You'll be inspired this week as you consider new directions for your life that lead to continued healing and hope.

## 1  TRY REFRAMING YOUR LIFE PICTURE

Have you ever seen the same photograph in two different frames? It's the same picture, but it can look completely different based on the frame around it.

The same idea can apply to difficult situations in life. People have a tendency to look at a situation and put a certain frame around it that says, "This is what it is. And this is what it means." But if you can look at the challenge from different angles and consider what possibilities exist, you can put a different frame on your circumstances.

This process is called *reframing*. You're not denying the reality of the circumstances or minimizing the difficulty involved. You're simply considering alternative interpretations and responses. This helps prevent the tunnel vision that often happens when life gets stressful. It allows you to see there is more to the story.

Here's an example of reframing: *Sara realizes she might lose the house in the divorce. To reframe, Sara* considers potential housing, lifestyle, and budget options, which opens up new possibilities for how she can respond to the situation.

Before you reframe your circumstances, let's practice a bit. How could you help a friend reframe the following situations?

1. **Your friend is down because she is going to be alone this weekend without her kids. Suggestions for reframing:**

2. **Your friend is frustrated because his divorce has left him short on money, so he can't go on his annual fishing trip. Suggestions for reframing:**

Now try reframing some of your current challenges. And ask your friends to help; they can often be more objective about your situation and help you consider options and perspectives that wouldn't occur to you.

## 2  HOW TRUTH CHANGES YOUR PERSPECTIVE

One way to reframe your situation is to make a distinction between what author and pastor Dwight McKissic calls "the facts" of your situation and "the truth."

If you want to be set free from your emotional condition (which is based on how you feel about the facts of your situation), move from focusing on the facts to focusing on the truths and promises of God, explains McKissic. Facts are an accurate description of your circumstances without consideration of God. "The fact is the doctor may have given you a disturbing diagnosis. The fact is you may be unemployed. But the truth is God said He would supply all your needs according to His riches in glory."

You become aware of the truth about your facts when you consider your circumstances in light of God's character and promises. Finding the truth requires getting more information from God's Word and receiving wise counsel before drawing conclusions solely from the raw data of your circumstances.

Fill in the chart below to help you start seeing how you can apply God's truth to the facts. If you don't know an applicable truth to place in the second column, pray for God's guidance as you search the Bible; ask a mature Christian friend or church leader; or try some online Bible study tools and search for keywords in the Bible. Download the chart at **divorcecare.org/my**.

| THE FACTS | THE TRUTH |
|---|---|
| I'm single and I feel lonely. | God is with me. He loves me. I have family and friends who love me. God will never leave me or forsake me. |
|  |  |

| THE FACTS | THE TRUTH |
|---|---|
|  |  |
|  |  |
|  |  |
|  |  |

*"We have to reorient ourselves around what really is truth, and that takes time. It's a process."*
– Elsa Kok Colopy

## 3  IS ALL THIS SUFFERING WORTH IT?

As you move along the path of suffering and healing, you'll find that you're becoming a new person. That can be scary, so you might try to hold on to familiar things, even though they're bad for you. But if you persevere in moving forward God's way, you'll find you're changing for the better.

## GOD'S MESSAGE TO YOU

*"**2** Consider it pure joy ... whenever you face trials of many kinds, **3** because you know that the testing of your faith produces perseverance. **4** Let perseverance finish its work so that you may be mature and complete, not lacking anything." (James 1:2–4)*

1. **According to today's verses, what comes from facing trials?**

2. **As you learn from your experiences and develop new character traits, you can reach a place where you function better than you have in the past. What growth have you experienced so far as you've begun the path of healing?**

3. **God values your spiritual development so much that He's willing to allow you to suffer to make progress in it. How would your view of suffering change if you valued your spiritual maturity as much as He does?**

## REMEMBER

- God doesn't waste suffering.

- "I've seen people who've been divorced for five years and are incredibly stable, strong, and deeply spiritual. They have a different perspective on life; they're much healthier than they were when they were married," says Christian author Chuck Milian. "I've seen people who've been divorced for 30 years [who haven't turned to God] and they're still angry, bitter, and cynical."

## WHAT ONLY YOU CAN OFFER

You have something so important—something other people in your church can't offer the same way you can. You're able to look a person who's hurting from divorce and separation in the eye and say: "I know it hurts. But you can make it through. I know, because I've been there." That reassurance can change the course of a person's journey.

### HOW CAN YOU SERVE?

God has equipped you with a story to tell and an experience to share. He promises to be with you and give you the tools you need every step of the way. "And God is able to bless you abundantly, so that in all things at all times, having all that you need, you will abound in every good work." (2 Corinthians 9:8)

An easy way to get started serving others is to help with DivorceCare. Your pastor or DivorceCare leader can help you understand where you're ready to serve based on where you are in your healing. You could start by helping with registration, greeting, snacks, or other supportive roles.

### WHY SERVE?

When you serve, you bless others and you are blessed.

Pam West, a DivorceCare leader, says, "I have been so blessed by being able to share my story. I want others to look at me now and say, 'There's hope.'" And Daniel Lehmann asks, "To watch people laugh, smile, and recognize they are not alone … how can you not want to be a part of that?"

Dr. Brad Hambrick, pastor, concludes, "If a church community is going to be a place where we walk well with those who go through the hardship of divorce, it's going to be because people like you have courage and vulnerability to share your story and build relationships."

*"When we give, we get back. It helps us heal."* – Alisa

## 5 LIVING DAILY WITH HOPE AND JOY

"The truth is our circumstances change all the time," says Dr. Crawford Loritts. "Ultimately, my joy comes out of knowing [God] and the fact that His purpose for my life will be completed."

## GOD'S MESSAGE TO YOU

*"6 Surely the righteous will never be shaken. … 7 They will have no fear of bad news; their hearts are steadfast, trusting in the LORD. 8 Their hearts are secure, they will have no fear; in the end they will look in triumph on their foes."* (Psalm 112:6–8)

*"May the God of hope fill you with all joy and peace as you trust in him, so that you may overflow with hope by the power of the Holy Spirit."* (Romans 15:13)

1. **During the darkest, shakiest, most fearful times, what does God promise to those who put their trust in Him, according to today's verses?**

2. **When the Bible speaks of being righteous, it's not something we achieve on our own. We receive Christ's righteousness, His goodness, as a gift when we believe in Him. Putting your trust in Him automatically places you in right standing with God because of what Jesus did. If you haven't already done that, what is keeping you from putting your full trust in God?**

See page ix to learn more about God's gift to you.

## REMEMBER

- You can have true joy.

- "Experiencing a relationship with God and beginning to trust Him in real ways takes time," says Elsa Kok Colopy. "It takes some prying your fingers loose from those broken things and taking steps forward. But know there's freedom on the other side of the bridge, and keep taking steps in that direction."

## MARY LOU'S STORY

*"Something that really helped me was taking my eyes off myself and serving others. With that came great healing. One way I serve is in our DivorceCare program at our church. I started with doing behind-the-scenes things, and now I'm a facilitator.*

*"It's amazingly rewarding to see people come in to DivorceCare nervous and in tears, and 13 weeks later be able to laugh and feel accepted. I can now let others know they're accepted and God still loves them—and He has a big plan for their life. He's going to take you somewhere if you partner with Him. Just hold on."*

# MY WEEKLY Journal

We've come a long way over the past few months. Use today's prompts to see how much you've changed in positive ways. Be encouraged by every step you've taken toward health and growth.

**1. The best change I've made so far is …**

**2. This has been helpful because …**

**3. An area I still need to work on is …**

**4. As I think about my skills and talents, I could be a blessing to others by …**

At some point, take time to review your past weekly journal entries. You'll probably be surprised by how much you and your perspective on your situation have changed by participating in DivorceCare.

## CHART YOUR PROGRESS

Place a check in the boxes to identify how you are feeling in each area this week: emotionally, physically, etc. Even better? Substitute a word or two to describe how you are doing.

| | REALLY BAD | OKAY | PRETTY GOOD | GREAT |
|---|---|---|---|---|
| **Emotionally** | | | | |
| **Physically** | | | | |
| **Spiritually** (closeness to God) | | | | |
| **Relationally** (closeness to others) | | | | |
| **How your life is in general** | | | | |

# FOR Parents

## *Myth: Children of divorce are destined for failure*
### Truth: There is HOPE for children of divorce

You might read the negative statistics about children of divorce and think your kids are doomed to fail. But it doesn't have to be that way.

Consider these two adult children of divorce: Brian Dollar and Dr. Brian Ranson. Dollar is a children's minister and the author of many children's ministry resources. Ranson worked his way through college and med school and is now a successful anesthesiologist in the Dallas, TX, area.

Many celebrities, actors, sports champions, gold medal winners, pastors, and other successful adults were raised in single-parent families. The fact is, kids in single-parent homes can (and do!) become strong, contributing members of society when they grow up.

### What helps them succeed?

In some ways, your children's experience with divorce or separation can help them become stronger individuals. They can learn from their heartache and struggles and use that knowledge to help others. Two results are common:

They can develop compassion:

- Divorce helps children develop sensitivity to others' suffering.

- They have empathy for children who are hurting, because they know how much it hurts to be uncomfortable in their life.

- Many adult children of divorce have compassion for others and display kindness because they want to help.

Second Corinthians 1:3–5 explains what can lead believing children to have such compassion for others:

"Praise be to the God and Father of our Lord Jesus Christ, the Father of compassion and the God of all comfort, who comforts us in all our troubles, so that we can comfort those in any trouble with the comfort we ourselves receive from God. For just as we share abundantly in the sufferings of Christ, so also our comfort abounds through Christ."

They're equipped for challenges:

- As children learn to handle difficult circumstances in healthy ways, they become ready for other challenges they will face in life.

- Their wounds heal over and become scars, which remind them of what they've made it through.

- Their sufferings prepare them to be used by God in others' lives.

James 1:3b–4 explains the hope that Christians can have that God can use their suffering to strengthen their character: "The testing of your faith produces perseverance. Let perseverance finish its work so that you may be mature and complete, not lacking anything."

### Brighter days ahead

With the right investment in your kids, your children can move forward in life's journey and enjoy a brighter future. Here are three good investments to start making today:

- **Study your kids:** Know who their friends are. Keep track of their online and social media activities. Take them to church and allow them to be active in God's family.

- **Pray with and for your kids:** Get into the habit of regularly praying with and for your children. Pray for them as often as you can.

- **Read to your kids:** Read God's Word to them. Encourage them to read it. Pray it over them. Cultivate in them a desire to know God through His Word. Planting this seed will produce wonderful fruit to help your children live an abundant life.

## Notes

1. US Department of Health and Human Services and US Department of Agriculture, *2015–2020 Dietary Guidelines for Americans*, 8th ed. (December 2015), http://health.gov/dietaryguidelines/2015/guidelines.

2. National Sleep Foundation, "National Sleep Foundation Recommends New Sleep Times," February 2, 2015, https://www.sleepfoundation.org/press-release/national-sleep -foundation-recommends-new-sleep-times.

3. American Academy of Sleep Medicine, "Healthy Sleep Habits," February 9, 2017, http://sleepeducation.org/essentials-in-sleep/healthy-sleep-habits.

4. American Heart Association, "Why Is Walking the Most Popular Form of Exercise?," January 10, 2017, https://www.heart.org/en/healthy-living/fitness/walking/why-is-walking -the-most-popular-form-of-exercise.

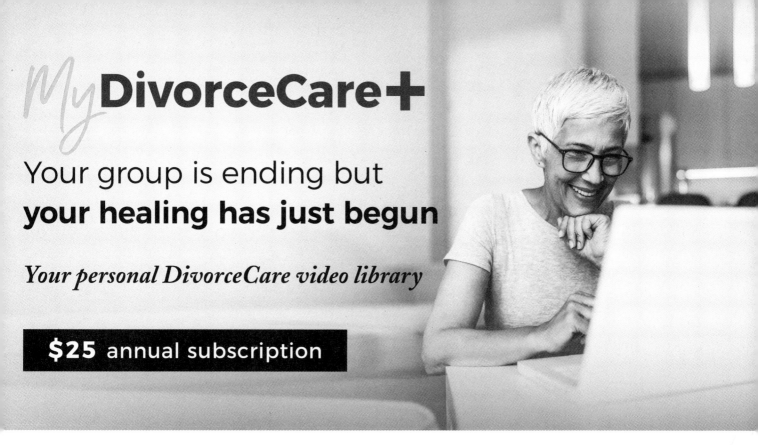

# WHAT'S NEXT?

As your 13-week group comes to a close, you have several options as to what you could do next. Consider these ideas:

## Repeat DivorceCare

If you repeat a 13-week cycle of DivorceCare, you'll catch things you missed the first time around. You'll also gain new and helpful insights because you'll be at a different level of growth and healing. Plus, you can encourage new group members and continue to build friendships with others.

## Volunteer to help with DivorceCare

Helping others helps you heal. Talk with your DivorceCare leader about ways you can help on the ministry team. For instance, you could help with registration, direct people in the parking lot, greet people coming in the door, arrange snacks, or help with publicity. And who knows? One day, you may even serve as a DivorceCare facilitator at this church or another church.

## Receive the "One Day at a Time" email encouragements

Gain strength for each day with these 365 short readings. These short messages arrive in your inbox with a tip, a teaching, or a note of encouragement to help you face each day. Sign up for these free daily email messages at **divorcecare.org/dailyemails**.

## Attend (or volunteer for) a Surviving the Holidays event

When Thanksgiving and Christmas come around, it can be stressful or just plain sad for some people after their divorce. DivorceCare hosts a Surviving the Holidays two-hour event, filled with practical advice on how to handle invitations, prying questions, awkward moments, kids' spending time with both parents, gift-giving, too-full schedules, finances, and more. If your group hasn't had its Surviving the Holidays event this year, talk with your DivorceCare leader about how you can help with this event.

## Connect with a Bible study or other small group

Consider joining a Bible study group or another small group or service opportunity sponsored by this church. Your group leaders can give you more information on what's offered and the groups that would be most beneficial to you. There is a lot of support and encouragement available if you take the first step.

## Go through Single & Parenting

If you're a single parent, look for the free Single & Parenting resource at MyDivorceCare (**divorcecare.org/my**). It's a 13-week program with online videos and a participant guide, offering tips, advice, and encouragement for the challenges of single parenting.

# BUDGET WORKSHEET

**D**o you find yourself without enough money to pay the bills? Spending more than you're earning? Not having money in the bank for emergencies? Just plain worrying about your finances? Keeping a budget is a way to help solve those problems. This worksheet will help you create a successful budget.

## Instructions

1. **Column A:** For one month, keep track of your income and expenses in each category. Doing this helps you keep from trying to guess your actual income and expenses.

2. **Column B:** After a month of tracking your income and expenses, create a budget in Column B. Do this by entering your anticipated income and by determining the maximum amount you need to, and can, spend in each category. (Note: Add categories as needed, and disregard those that don't apply.)

3. **Column C:** Record the difference by subtracting Column A from B. This will let you know when your income and/or expenses get out of whack.

## Online version

This worksheet is available as a downloadable, interactive spreadsheet at **divorcecare.org /my/budget**. Discover the benefits of keeping a budget!

# INCOME

| Monthly Income | COLUMN A<br>AMOUNT I RECEIVED THIS MONTH | COLUMN B<br>BUDGETED AMOUNT | COLUMN C<br>DIFFERENCE (COLUMN B – A) |
|---|---|---|---|
| Your salary (after taxes) | | | |
| Unemployment benefits | | | |
| Welfare payments | | | |
| Child support/alimony | | | |
| Other – | | | |
| Other – | | | |
| Total income | | | |

# EXPENSES

| Monthly Expenses | COLUMN A<br>AMOUNT I SPENT THIS MONTH | COLUMN B<br>BUDGETED AMOUNT (I CAN'T GO OVER THIS!) | COLUMN C<br>DIFFERENCE (COLUMN B – A) |
|---|---|---|---|
| **HOUSING/UTILITIES** | | | |
| Mortgage/rent | | | |
| Insurance/taxes | | | |
| Electricity | | | |
| Water/sewer | | | |
| Gas | | | |
| Trash | | | |
| Telephone (landline) | | | |
| Cell phone | | | |
| Cable | | | |
| Internet | | | |
| Home maintenance | | | |
| Yard maintenance | | | |
| Cleaning supplies | | | |
| Other – | | | |
| **Total housing/utilities** | | | |
| **FOOD** | | | |
| Groceries | | | |
| Eating out | | | |
| Coffee/vending machine | | | |
| Special events | | | |
| **Total food** | | | |

| Monthly Expenses (cont.) | COLUMN A AMOUNT I SPENT THIS MONTH | COLUMN B BUDGETED AMOUNT (I CAN'T GO OVER THIS!) | COLUMN C DIFFERENCE (COLUMN B – A) |
|---|---|---|---|
| **VEHICLE(S)/TRANSPORTATION** | | | |
| Payments | | | |
| Gas | | | |
| Oil change | | | |
| Insurance/taxes/license | | | |
| Maintenance/repairs | | | |
| Public transit/parking/tolls | | | |
| **Total vehicle(s)/transportation** | | | |
| **INSURANCE** | | | |
| Medical | | | |
| Dental | | | |
| Life | | | |
| Other – | | | |
| **Total insurance** | | | |
| **MEDICAL EXPENSES** | | | |
| Doctor | | | |
| Dentist | | | |
| Prescription drugs | | | |
| Other – | | | |
| **Total medical expenses** | | | |
| **DEBTS** | | | |
| Credit card 1 – | | | |
| Credit card 2 – | | | |
| Credit card 3 – | | | |
| Loans | | | |
| **Total debts** | | | |
| **CHILDREN** | | | |
| Child care | | | |
| School books/supplies | | | |
| School lunch | | | |
| School uniform(s)/tuition | | | |
| Field trips/misc. fees | | | |
| Sport(s) & equipment | | | |
| Lessons | | | |
| Club/group/hobbies | | | |
| Other – | | | |
| **Total children** | | | |

| Monthly Expenses (cont.) | AMOUNT I SPENT THIS MONTH | BUDGETED AMOUNT (I CAN'T GO OVER THIS!) | DIFFERENCE (COLUMN B – A) |
|---|---|---|---|
| **ADULT EDUCATION** | | | |
| Tuition/fees | | | |
| Books/materials | | | |
| **Total adult education** | | | |
| **ENTERTAINMENT** | | | |
| Movies/games/hobbies | | | |
| Vacation(s) | | | |
| Music/books | | | |
| Other – | | | |
| **Total entertainment** | | | |
| **GIVING** | | | |
| Church | | | |
| Charity/community | | | |
| **Total giving** | | | |
| **MISCELLANEOUS** | | | |
| Clothes | | | |
| Haircuts | | | |
| Toiletries/cosmetics | | | |
| Pets | | | |
| Gym/exercise | | | |
| Subscriptions | | | |
| Other – | | | |
| **Total miscellaneous** | | | |
| **SAVINGS** | | | |
| Money to set aside (emergency, large purchases, etc.) | | | |
| Christmas and birthdays | | | |
| Retirement/investments | | | |
| College | | | |
| **Total savings** | | | |
| **Total Expenses** (total amount for all 12 expense categories – housing, food, etc.) | | | |

# SUMMARY

| | | | |
|---|---|---|---|
| Total income (from top of p. 138) | | | |
| Total expenses | | | |
| **Income minus expenses** | | | |